The Way of the Traveler's H.E.A.R.T.

Experience the Fullness and Variety of Life...
With or Without a Passport

Julie A. Zolfo

Columbus, Ohio

The views and opinions expressed in this book are solely those of the author and do not reflect the views or opinions of Gatekeeper Press. Gatekeeper Press is not to be held responsible for and expressly disclaims responsibility of the content herein.

The Way of the Traveler's H.E.A.R.T.: Experience the Fullness and Variety of Life...With or Without a Passport

Published by Gatekeeper Press
2167 Stringtown Rd, Suite 109
Columbus, OH 43123-2989
www.GatekeeperPress.com

Copyright © 2021 by Julie A. Zolfo

All rights reserved. Neither this book, nor any parts within it may be sold or reproduced in any form or by any electronic or mechanical means, including information storage and retrieval systems, without permission in writing from the author. The only exception is by a reviewer, who may quote short excerpts in a review.

ISBN (paperback): 9781662917158
eISBN: 9781662919473

I dedicate this book to all travelers – with or without a passport - who favor following newer signposts towards the unknown, the uncharted, and the unexperienced rather than the old roads to comfort, conformity, and certainty.

By integrating travel's most invaluable lessons of courage, perseverance, responsibility, openness and the acceptance of life, others, and yourself, you significantly increase your chances to experience a rich, purposeful life, daily.

May this book help you dare to live differently.

CONTENTS

Acknowledgments	1
Greetings from the Author	5
You are Here	7
The Legend: Discover the H.E.A.R.T. Elements	9
H	11
Reflection on H	31
E	37
Reflection on E	71
A	73
Reflection on A	93
R	93
Reflection on R	133
T	131
Reflection on T	151
26 Ways to Keep Your Traveler's Heart Beating Everyday	155
Unpack Your Traveler's H.E.A.R.T.	157
About the Author	159

ACKNOWLEDGMENTS

TO MY MOM, Carol Zolfo, thank you for your unwavering love, for encouraging me to follow my dreams, for being readily available to dust me off when I trip and fall, and for saying those extra needed prayers. I love you to the stars and back.

To my dad, Frank Zolfo, thank you for investing in my happiness and success. From YMCA Princess trips to Sunday football games to speech rewrites, house repairs, politics, finances, career advice and cleaning tips …there is nothing we cannot speak about. I want you to know that every moment I get to learn and just experience you are moments I treasure. I am honored and blessed that God chose you to be my dad.

To my sister Deanna, thank you for being my biggest cheerleader, dial-in counselor, and first-ever friend.

To my brother Frankie, thank you for filling my heart with so many cherished childhood memories and the even bigger memories I am making with you and your family.

To my sister-in-laws, Been and Pattay. You may call yourselves the outlaws and add-ons, but in my heart, you are life-time members of the Fab 5.

Thank you, Alyssa and my three nephews Sean, Frankie, and Jack, for fueling my heart with love and joy. It is an honor to be your aunt and Godmother.

To my cousins Pete, Robert, John, and Michael, I hold you in my heart as my 4 other brothers. I love each of you and our incredible family members that you added: Kim, Tina, Kierstyn, PJ, Arianna, Connor, Marlena, Ron, and Judy.

To My Aunt Patty and Aunt Judy, thank you for taking a strong interest in my life and supporting all my dreams. I treasure your love.

To my hall of fame angels in heaven, including Nana, Grandpa, Grandma, my Godfather, Aunt Mary, Uncle John, Cousin William, Aunt Bernie, Madeleine, and Stu, thank you for being my constant protectors. Your presence and love remain alive in my heart and mind.

To my special roommates over the years - Terri, Karin, Halina, Grainne, and Christine - thank you for being there in good times and hard times. The twists and turns, the ups and downs have made for an interesting and thrilling ride.

To my PIER 39 and Greens Sport Bar Family members in San Francisco, I love and adore you all. Thank you for the treasured memories and lasting friendships.

To Susan Giulini-Bamberger and Cindy Caruso Aquila, thank you for opening new doors for my career. You significantly changed the trajectory of my life and life's work thanks to working at Turner Broadcasting, Double-Click and Citigroup. As a bonus I got to keep each of you as life-long friends. Love you both to pieces.

To Janet Attwood, thank you for being one of my greatest mentors and teachers. Thanks to you, the Passion Test process, and the global Passion Test family, not only is my life richer and more abundant, I get to inspire people all over the world to create and experience fulfilling careers and personal lives, too.

Thank you to the travel companies Country Walkers, Cross Cultural Solutions, Monkey Tours and Active Adventures. I could have not made this journey without your journeys.

Thanks to my guide, Bishnu, Elder, and Joseph in Nepal, Peru, and India, respectively. Trekking mountains and experiencing new cultures with each of you made an imprint on my heart that has stayed. I continue to carry your spirit wherever my happy feet lead me.

Thank you, Glenn - my buddy and my pal – for helping to water my adventure seed over three decades ago.

Hugs to all my friends and angels who have been there and walked with me along the journey.

Thank you, iPEC and Jenn Barley, my master trainer and dear friend. My required coaching presentation in 2008, ironically created the initial framework for the Traveler's H.E.A.R.T. concept.

Thank you, Monique Redmon, for bringing me into your Hikerbabes Community. The regularly scheduled hikes have helped me to explore new trails while making wonderful connections and new friendships – like the one I have with Gwen Harris (and the Menopause Support Group). I just love this community of adventurous and supportive women.

To the Transformation Travel Council, I am grateful to be an Active Ally Member as we work together to take the message of meaningful and purposeful travel experiences to the next level.

To Barbara Breyer and Anjl Rodee, thank you for contributing your photoshop and illustrator expertise to help get this book across the finish line. Your generosity and friendship are truly treasured. I owe you both big time!!!!

To Cheryl, thank you for believing in me, back in 2010.

To Christine, thank you for your unwavering friendship, support, and love. God bless you ten-fold!

Thank you, Kim Eldredge, for being the lighthouse I so desperately needed for my book to come ashore. As my book coach, your expertise, guidance, dedication, helped ensure my message of adventure would be heard and my dream of becoming a published author become a reality.

And finally, to Kathleen Leary. Without fail, for 39 years, you have been my lifeline in good times and bad. Last year was no exception. You held my hand over 13 months and together we had our own adventure that brought the Traveler's H.E.A.R.T. to life. Your leadership, your expertise, your intuition, and YOUR heart are now embedded in every page and are part of this book's legacy. I am forever grateful and so proud of what we have accomplished.

GREETINGS FROM THE AUTHOR

"AND SO THE adventure begins…" These are the first words I wrote in my first travel journal in December 1997. I don't think I knew exactly what I meant at the time. Today, just over twenty years later, I have a better idea of what I meant, but I am still experiencing and learning. I am still on the adventure. In the twenty-three years since I wrote those words, I have climbed (and am still climbing) mountains – not just physically, but also metaphorically. There have been peaks and valleys, some very high and some incredibly low. I have learned a lot about myself, about others, and about life. My adventures have taught me how to stop and observe, both as a traveler on the top of a mountain and as a transformational coach down in the trenches. Through my travels, my life experiences, and my coaching certificates and teachings, I have created The Traveler's H.E.A.R.T. – a philosophy and mindset for daily living that aligns with five wisdoms and fuels five desires that drive our choices and decisions.

And as I stand on the newest mountain in my life – having moved to Bend, Oregon, where hiking and mountain climbing are a way of life – I take time to honor the guides I have had in my life and on my travels. I have been lucky enough to walk with some amazing people through the mountains and valleys of New Zealand, Southeast Asia, South America, and my own backyard. I am also humbled and honored to have supportive guides in my life, including my parents, my teachers, and some amazing strangers who have come in and out of my life.

If you open your eyes, you will find guides in all areas of your life – from the very old (like the woman I met in India who told me I was "all closed off" as I sat with my arms and legs crossed), to the very young (like my five-year-old nephew whose excitement and naivety helps me to see the world in a fresh new way).

But I also found a guide I was not expecting. The guide who I now realize had been there all along. The guide whose intuition and instincts have kept me safe and pushed me further than I ever imagined going. That guide is me.

And that guide has led me to the top of the world. My world.

Through all of my travels, I have learned that all roads lead to home, whether that home is a physical structure, people in your life, or a place you carry in your heart. When you get where you are going, you know that you have found and reached your true home.

Thank you for picking up my book, reading my stories, and taking my journey with me. My hope is for you to find the guide who leads you on a path of your own journey.

YOU ARE HERE

LIKE A MAP hanging on the wall at the highway rest stop with a "You are Here" icon, you are here in your life. Whether that is traveling the world or getting up each day to go to work, you are here. Is that "here" where you are supposed to be? Is that "here" where you want to be? The wisdoms and desires associated with each letter in The Traveler's H.E.A.R.T. help you figure that out.

The Traveler's H.E.A.R.T. concept is an approach to living a life filled with connection, curiosity, courage, clarity, and co-creating. The Traveler's H.E.A.R.T. book is filled with stories about my life and travels, and how each letter of the H.E.A.R.T. concept has led me to where I am today.

Through my work as a transformational life coach, I intuitively synthesized my years of education and training, along with my life experiences and professional expertise, to create the Traveler's H.E.A.R.T. concept. After receiving a bachelor's degree in business marketing from Bentley University, I returned to the classroom years later to earn my certification from the Institute for Professional Excellence in Coaching (iPEC). My certifications and training from iPEC include certified professional coach, energy leadership master practitioner, and a CORE transition dynamics specialist. I continued to invest in my coaching skills by enrolling in Tony Robbins' official school of training after attending one of his fire-walk seminars. Now, I am also a Robbins Madanes strategic intervention life coach and am certified to distribute and coach on the MHSEQi.2.0 emotional intelligence assessment. In 2010, I became a certified facilitator for the Passion Test, Passion Test for Business, and

Mastery of Self-Love courses created by Janet Attwood, as well as a master trainer for the Passion Test Train the Trainer certification courses. I have studied under psychotherapists and astrologists Debra Silverman and Lada Duncheva. I have over 2,000 hours of astrology continuing education and training in Western, Esoteric, and Vedic Astrology.

And I am a master traveler of the world.

I combined my love of travel with my coaching skills to create The Traveler's H.E.A.R.T. When people travel, they often come back to their lives refreshed and full of wonder. They look at the world through colorful lenses tinted by their experiences. With refreshed eyes, they see more options available to them and are curious about those new possibilities. Then something happens that brings their focus back to their pre-travel mindset. They shut down, stop looking for the next new experience, and return to the monotony of their pre-travel life.

However, it doesn't have to be that way. With the Wisdoms and Desires of The Traveler's H.E.A.R.T., I help you navigate that experience by guiding you on how to step up and explore new possibilities, step in and experiment without expectations, and step out and expand beyond what you know.

When we travel, we aren't afraid to try new things and live, even for a few days, outside of our comfort zone. Sometimes we don't recognize the person living that life, but we like how it feels. With the Traveler's H.E.A.R.T., you can continue to explore, experiment, and expand your life, even after the plane has landed and you have packed away the suitcases. Remember that you are here. Right here. Right where you are meant to be.

THE LEGEND:

DISCOVER THE H.E.A.R.T. ELEMENTS

OUR MOST FULFILLING choices – those that create our current life experience – come not from focusing on what we know, but from deliberately experimenting with new thoughts, ideas, beliefs, concepts, and actions constantly and consistently. This single focus keeps our soul alive and well.

A seasoned traveler knows that change, transition, and the unknown will be part of their experience. They not only embrace these experiences; they often seek them for fun. Why? So, they can know what's on the other side of what they don't yet know!

Most people I know don't view their everyday lives as a travel experience. Instead, they get caught up in the mundane, the logical, the practical, the shoulds, and the self-imposed restrictions of everyday life. I can't let that happen to you any longer.

On the next page are the elements which constitute my coaching concept The Traveler's H.E.A.R.T. There are 5 Wisdoms to guide you and 5 Desires to help fulfill you… with or without a passport.

Julie A. Zolfo

Wisdom: Home is a Sensation of Belonging, Not a Destination of Belongings
Desire: Connection

Wisdom: Experience Without Expectations
Desire: Curiosity

Wisdom: Adversity Accelerates Self-Evolution
Desire: Courage

Wisdom: Recalculate What Matters Most
Desire: Clarity

Wisdom: Trust That Plans Always Change and Just F.L.O.W.
Desire: Co-create

WISDOM:

HOME IS A SENSATION OF BELONGING, NOT A DESTINATION OF BELONGINGS

DESIRE:

CONNECTION

ONE ORDINARY DAY in August 1997, I went to the mailbox and found a large white envelope addressed to Julie Zolfo (me). It was from Country Walkers. It was real.

A few months earlier, I'd filled out one of those perforated postcards in a magazine while waiting for my hair appointment at Dante's salon in San Francisco. Country Walkers promised travelers the local experience through walking tours. The excursion that sparked my interest was a twelve-day walking and hiking tour of New Zealand's South Island. I was looking for a way to celebrate turning thirty, and as I'd recently read on the company's website, "When you explore the world on foot, you give yourself a gift."

And that is exactly what I set out to do: give myself a gift. Like every other person in corporate America, I was allotted two weeks for vacation. I was very aware that not everyone has the advantage of taking those two weeks back-to-back, and that not everyone has the luxury of flying off to Christchurch, New Zealand for a walking tour. I understood that this was something special, and I was intent on treating it that way.

From the moment I read the ad in the magazine, I put the plan into motion. I booked the twelve-day trip for the end of December into January. My office in San Francisco closed for the holiday break, so I went home to New Jersey for Christmas. My family embraced my travel plans, and my gifts were all travel related, including a new camcorder from my dad to video my adventures.

It was wonderful that my family was supporting my adventure. I was already on a different path from them –except my father. I seemed to be following in his corporate footsteps. At twenty-nine, I was the first woman in my family to have a college degree, but I was the only one still single and driven on climbing further up the corporate ladder that my big Italian family considered success.

Though my family merely saw the New Zealand walking tour as something fun, it was more than a vacation for me. Even so, what I thought it was and what it turned out to be were two completely different things.

I thought it was
- My first solo trip,
- My first time traveling out of the country on my own,
- My first trip that was an adventure and not a vacation,
- My first-time touring with a group of people I didn't know, and
- A hike.

It turned out to be an experience which taught me the following lessons:
- I have a place in the world. (I found that place, and I found myself.)
- My soul is filled through travel, and I need to experience it as often as possible.
- No matter where you travel in the world, you can belong.
- The strangers that you meet, either traveling companions or locals, all have the potential to leave a large imprint on your life. Each new person is a new connection.
- I can climb mountains big and small.

The fun part of writing this book was having actual correspondence and handwritten journals from my adventures. I keep just about everything. (I'm not a hoarder, just a memory keeper.) I even kept the welcome letter that confirmed my travel arrangements and the walking tour accommodations.

Dear Julie,

We are delighted to have you join us on **The New Zealand – The South Island 12-Day Exploration** *starting on December 30, 1997 through January 10, 1998. Thank you for your reservation and deposit. Enclosed, please find the following...*

- Meeting Point: Cotswold Hotel, Christchurch @ 930 a.m.
- Departure Point: Queenstown Airport @ mid-morning
- Terrain: Easy-to-moderate with strenuous options, 5-13 miles per day, 4-7 hours each day
- Accommodations: hotels, inns, and wilderness lodges, private baths for 11 nights
- Meals: All meals included except for one dinner and one lunch

The letter and the information in the packet provided all the details of the trip. They'd accounted for every last minute and all necessities. I felt safe traveling around the world alone because professionals were handling all the details.

This letter from the Country Walkers told me where I would meet the tour guides and where I would depart from. It didn't tell me I would meet thirteen people who would start as strangers but who, through sharing moments, meals, and memories, would depart as comrades.

12/27/97 Saturday

And so, the adventure begins....and it has been nonstop ever since. New Jersey! It's 3:55 p.m. and I'm sitting at SFO watching the Denver and Jacksonville Wildcard game! My flight to L.A. begins boarding at 4:30 p.m. The bags are checked all the way through to

Christchurch… it's a bit worrisome, however. I've packed an extra shirt and underwear just in case the luggage is delayed! As I'm waiting for the flight, I'm writing notes to everyone to thank them for a wonderful holiday! Christmas was perfect this year! I believe I cried more leaving Mom's house on Thursday than the day I left to move to San Francisco. However, the feelings I was experiencing were just pure joy. I love hanging with the family. It is my favorite pastime!!

The first line of this journal entry sums up not only my trip, but every day of my life since New Zealand. "And so, the adventure begins…" It is funny that I say it so early in the trip. I hadn't even left America. I was sitting at an airport, watching American football. Maybe the first line should have been, "And so the excitement begins…"

12/29/97 Monday

8:45 a.m. (New Zealand time – 13 hours ahead of the West Coast and 16 hours ahead of the East Coast of North America)
Good Morning! It's 8:45 a.m., 12/29, and I'm on my last leg of flights. We're approx. 20 minutes from landing in Christchurch! Feeling a bit sluggish, but the inflight breakfast will hold me over – not to mention the 2 cups of coffee. No major problems thus far. The bags arrived from SFO to Auckland… very relieved!

I picked up a few brochures in Auckland about Christchurch and Queenstown. (The captain just came on and mentioned that Christchurch is 10°C (10 x 2 + 30 = 50°F). A cloud covering is blocking any view of the island… so much for the great window seat!

Thinking of a city tour this afternoon once I settle into the hotel. Looking forward to meeting up with the tour group. So far, the journey has been a bit lonely. Met a nice guy from L.A. on the flight from LAX to Auckland. He works for GES in Orange

County. I know his last name is Turner. He is on his way to Brisbane for 3 weeks… No love connection above the clouds. The sun is shining. Another great day. Write more later about my 1st day.

5:45 p.m.
Just returned from a ½ day city tour of Christchurch and Canterbury and was greeted by a note on my floor from my older sister, Deanna. It was as if she was actually here! It felt great!

I was surprised to learn how much England had an influence on Christchurch.

The drive to the outskirts of town looked like Marin and the Oakland Hills in California. (I can understand why 80% of Californians travel within California… everything's there… mountains, beaches, cities, and suburbs.) Attempted to use the camcorder, but something went wrong… I'll read the directions tonight. I'm heading out for some Mexican food, bed early, and meet the group tomorrow… Can't wait!

That day. Three days after I left my home. Two days into the trip to a foreign country. I find it interesting that I mention I am lonely and miss home. The landscape of Christchurch reminded me of the towns I lived near in northern California. It strikes me now that I traveled halfway around the world to experience something new, and I found something so similar to home that I felt a sense of connection.

Also, this is when I should have written, "And so the adventure begins…"

12/30/97 Tuesday
8:45 a.m.

Great night's sleep. Ready for the adventure! Looking out the window, it's still looking gray today, but it's warmer than yesterday. Last night before I came back to my room, I stopped by the front desk to ask where Country Walkers was meeting in the morning. She told me she had no record of the company... Oh?!? Now it's 45 minutes before the group is scheduled to meet and I'm still not quite sure what's happening. (Keep smiling... it's all part of the adventure.) God, please watch over me just a little extra today so everything starts ok. Thanks!

Trust the process. Trust the process. Trust God. Trust the process. Breathe.

12/31/97
7:45 a.m.

Good Morning! Had the most incredible experience on Day 1 of the New Zealand Adventure! It's everything I wished it to be and so much more! Met with Ed and Nikki (escorts) and the group at 9:30 am. Surprisingly 80% of the group is from California. We began our journey at 10:30 am and headed towards Arthur's Pass. After a two-hour drive, we stopped for a wonderful picnic lunch at the base of the hiking trail. Day 1, I chose to do the challenging trail – everyone but 2 people did it! We walked 5 miles through breathtaking beech tree forests! What's so great is that our escort Ed is an ecology major. He knows everything about the New Zealand islands. Can't wait to show the video. When we finished, Nikki met us at the other side of the mountain. Next was the Wilderness Lake. "Choice"

The place is beautiful! As soon as we arrived, we headed toward the farm to watch the dogs gather the sheep... fascinating! Then the ultimate New Zealand experience... I helped shear a sheep... "Choice"

I am sharing a room with Cydney; she is from Pacifica, California. Our room has a large sliding glass window that overlooks the mountains.

Dinner was another pleasant surprise. Bouillabaisse, Canterbury rack of lamb, veggies, and warm apple tart with vanilla ice cream (low fat?). The average New Zealander consumes 2 scoops of ice cream per day... I love this place!

9:10 a.m.

Sunshine and blue skies today! We're heading out for a 7-hour hike! This is incredible... Everyone needs to do this!

6:15 p.m.

Just awoke from a great hour-long nap. Today, the group walked through the Warmakariri Valley for a 6-mile hike (felt more like 8-10). Lots of beech forest, open land. Incredible peaks and great conversations. I found a quote I'm not sure mom's heard: "We don't attract what we want; rather we attract who we are." Pretty powerful... SLOGAN FOR 1998!

While walking today, I couldn't help but reflect on 1997... It was definitely a year of growth! As I prepare to enter my 30th year, I have to say I'm pretty impressed with my accomplishments. God has truly blessed me and for that I'm extremely THANKFUL! Marybeth said another great slogan on the trails today that I'd like to end this page, day, and year on. "If PRAYER is talking to God, then INTUITION is God speaking to us."

HAPPY NEW YEAR! I'm listening!!!! At least I'm learning to listen better!!

Rereading my journal, I can't believe the experiences I had on the very first day. I look at my pictures, and I see my excitement and my readiness to participate. It wasn't a sense of adventure; it was a sense of belonging because our guides made us feel part of a close-knit group. Maybe being strangers, most of whom lived in the same country and same state, helped the instant bonding. Or it was the kindred spirit of being hikers interested in exploring a new country. The reason didn't matter because the camaraderie was instant.

All the hikers were older than me. The next youngest was my roommate, Cydney. She was ten years my senior. However, it never felt like there was an age difference. Our travel hobby and the willingness to explore and learn kept us a tight, respectful group.

I also have to laugh at how we lived in the lap of luxury during this trek. How did we even hike the next morning with our bellies so full?

This next section wasn't in my actual New Zealand Journal. I put it together from notes, pictures, and memories. I can still feel myself under the stars as the clock struck midnight. I can still hear the music from that night. Being under the stars and recognizing the constellations that were upside down from where I lived in North America gave me a feeling of warmth and comfort, and the knowledge that I can feel at home anywhere under the same bright stars.

> *At 9:30 p.m., all the guests in the Wilderness Lodge were invited to meet in the Black Ranger Conference room. The hosts of the lodge, Anne Saunders, and Gerry McSweeney had arranged a special New Year's night walk for all the guests to experience stargazing. Surprisingly, not many guests took advantage of the night walk. In total, there were about 12 of us. This allowed for a more intimate and quieter experience.*

During the walk, we had flashlights or head lamps. It wasn't until we shut off the devices that we were able to experience the night sky. I had never in my life seen that many stars. There were thousands and thousands of shining white lights above us. It was truly magical and transcendent, especially when I finally spotted Orion in the night sky, upside down.

As a kid, I loved going to the Hayden Planetarium in New York City with my dad to learn about the sky, the stars, and the universe beyond planet Earth. I remember many nights growing up in New Jersey when I would lie in my bed, which was positioned under the windowsill, and stare for hours at the moon and night sky, hoping to see a shooting star or something just as magical. My favorite constellation was and continues to be Orion, the Hunter.

When I went back east for Christmas, prior to this trip, I noticed my Dad still had the atlases and Encyclopedia Britannica set I used in the 1980s for all my school reports. I found the page with the constellations of the Southern Hemisphere. I'd photocopied that page and brought it with me to New Zealand so I would know the Southern Cross when looking into the night sky.

When the walk ended, we moved to a field behind the property where the owners had set up blankets and a few folding chairs.

After 30 minutes of quiet, one of the guests, a gentleman from Germany, started to play soft instrumental music on his guitar. How could my life get any better than this, I thought. I was living in a dream. Within moments of him strumming his strings, tears streamed down my cheeks and onto my sweatshirt.

"Excuse me," I said to the woman sitting on the blanket in front of me. I saw her walk in with him earlier, so I made the bold assumption they were a couple. "Do you know what song he is playing?"

When she turned to face me, she, too, had tears rolling down her cheeks. The woman replied in a low, soft, sweet voice, in broken English. "It's called Innerhalb - in English you would say 'within.'"

"Within?" I asked with great curiosity, while instinctively pointing my finger towards my heart.

"Ja," she said, her head nodding.

For the next hour, I sat in awe of the moment, feeling a strange nothing and everything at the same time. Was this what an outer body experience feels like? I continued to sit in the grass field, frozen in stillness as a fountain of deep joy bubbled up, warming every cell in my body. Sitting under that New Year's Eve starry sky, beneath the famous Southern Cross and my favorite constellation, Orion (who was amusingly positioned upside down), I sensed something magical was waiting for me at the strike of the new year.

Back in my room, Cydney had already fallen asleep. But I couldn't. Instead, I continued to gaze into the night sky. It was as if I was having an astral travel experience while I was awake.

Remember the scene in the first Superman movie with Christopher Reeve, when he takes Lois Lane on a night fly-over? As a kid, I had dreams that I could fly just like that. It would always be at night in my dream as I flew over millions of city lights below me. Tonight, looking out my window into the New Zealand sky, I could hear the song "Could You Read my Mind?" playing and I saw myself flying. I had never been more sober and yet felt as if I was having the ultimate psychedelic mushroom trip... But it was all real.

1/1/1998
9:45 p.m.
What a choice day! It started with the sun shining and then continued with wonderful walks, lots of laughs, and tons of fun.

The morning walk was an easy 1-hour walk through the high country of Arthur's Pass. One gentleman, Richard, has been very sick up to this day and was still having difficulties with this easy walk. I would not be surprised if he and his wife leave early.

After the walk, we drove 45 minutes to our second hike through a rain forest... I liked this a lot! Ed is so well educated on New Zealand; he is a pure delight to be with. He makes the trip. I'm learning so much.

The last hike brought us to Greymouth, and we strolled through another forest before heading to Kings Motor Lodge... Nothing like the Wilderness Lodge! We were spoiled staying there our first night! Had some excitement with the hairdryers and outlets in the room. They were sparking and flaming. No hair dryer this evening.

Spoke to Deana and Patty at 6:00 pm New Zealand time, and they were happy to hear from me as I, they. I want everyone to do a trip like this. It's an incredible experience. I don't know how I'll top this New Year's next year... Slow down, Jules! Let's get through 1998... Live for today! PS – Quote of the Day: "I don't want to be a nurse or a purse..." referring to a relationship with a man – Cydney

When I reread my journal and hear myself using the New Zealand phrase "Choice," I can't help but smile how, after just three days in the country, I already felt comfortable and connected and was growing in confidence.

This is a very important journal entry for me to look back and read. I see how I called home at the exact time my sister and her wife were celebrating the New Year beginning in their sphere of the world. It was paramount to me halfway around the world to connect with my family and feel a thread of the world I came from.

I wish I could take my younger self aside and whisper in her ear, "Don't worry. Don't rush things. Just wait! You think this experience on New Year's Eve can't be topped? Just wait! 1998 is a year of planning for an even bigger hike. And it might be safe to say that your New Year 1999 doesn't start until mid-January. 1999 is a new year and a semi-new you. But don't think about that. Live 1998 first!"

I love the January 2 journal entry. At one point, it was a letter to my mother. I don't think she ever read it, but she will now. I traveled to another country. I walked many miles up and down mountains, in woods, along beaches, and through towns. And I traveled within to find myself. Did I need to go outside into nature to go inside?

1/2/1998
9:30 p.m.
Started slow this morning… didn't meet the group for breakfast. I had a dream that somehow the Jets were in the playoff… a prime example of fantasy football. We left the hotel at 8:30 am. The first walk was a 4-mile walk along the beach at Port Elizabeth.

At one point, I got a bit emotional thinking about you, Mom. I want you to know that I've really heard you over the last few years, and I'm so thankful for all your advice! I don't think I'd be so peaceful without all your insights into personal development and healing. Often, I give dad more credit, but it's you who has taught me to teach myself how to be at peace. Thank you! I owe you my happiness.

After the walk, we stopped along a beautiful beach for lunch. As Nicky and Ed were setting lunch, a few of us went to pick rocks. The second walk was through a tourist spot, which was beautiful – a rock formation. The 3rd walk was along a limestone forest area. All together, we walked over 8 miles. NOT BAD!

I'm having such a great time! I'm so glad I'm here. Don't know what I'd be doing at home. I was truly placed here... Looking forward to what's next.

Thanks for another great day!

Today Carol from Ohio and I had an inspiring conversation about women staying too long at their jobs. God, is it time to leave my job at PIER 39? In my heart, I'm beginning to think it is, as you say in your prayers to me today.

My guidance from God is just what I need to know – when I need to know it.

Keep me open to hear you!

The conversation with Carol confirmed for me that age was not a demographic that mattered when out on the trails. Travel – vacation – is a commonality. Also, our conversation about staying too long in a job was the match that created the spark that lit the bomb that would soon go off in my heart and head.

1/5/1998
5:00 p.m.
Haven't written for a while. There's so much to share! Since the beautiful beach walk, life has changed so dramatically. Next to report... Hokitika was a stopping point to buy jade. I really wanted to buy myself a ring, but nothing stood out. I did purchase Deanna a great jade pin, which I'll give her for her birthday. Debating whether to get Frankie, my younger brother, a jade

necklace. I think he'll like it. In Hokitika, there was a sign for Underwater World... oh dear! I ran!

Then it was off to Fox Glacier, but not before stopping at Wangahui Creek for a choice tramp on the actual glacier! As we arrived in Fox Glacier, Ed was so excited to see old friends. He worked as a guide on the Glacier for a few summers. (He's great!)

Without much time to unpack, Ed took several of us to a vista point to see Mt. Tasman, Mt. Cook, and the other ranges. Breathtaking! After a so-so dinner, Cydney, Carol, and I went to look at the glowworms.

As I sit here and recall the experiences we've been encountering, the most important thing is happening within all of us. Somehow, we know that our lives are different because of this experience. It's so amazing! Looking out into the ocean today, I was having a conversation with God on what he has next for me. I can only imagine. There is so much living to do! Where do I begin to go next? I'm looking for a big change.

It's time for BIGGER THINGS! My job at PIER 39 is a steppingstone for me. I do have so much more to offer the world! I haven't been living. Enough... No more!

There are signs everywhere. But I think I was too young to notice them. My eyes, heart, and mind were not open enough yet. In this last journal entry, I was thinking about quitting my job. I was thinking about moving to New Zealand.

Maybe seeing the Underwater World sign was an actual sign from God for which I had been asking. I had been part of a team responsible for the marketing and grand opening events for the Underwater World Aquarium in San Francisco. My vacation to New Zealand was my chance to get away from it all. If I had been open to receiving signs, maybe I would have noticed how I was part of something bigger – something global. If I had been open to receiving signs, maybe I would have made the universe's connection to home when I was halfway around the world. Instead of thinking "I can't get away from work," maybe I should have been thinking "Oh, look. A part of home is here with me."

In the years since this trip, I have learned to look and listen. But the choices I made in 1998 and 1999 made me the person I am today. The mountains I have climbed both on the planet, and in my life, have been high and low. And yet, I am still stepping into the unknown, just with more confidence, curiosity, and ease. Thank you, New Zealand.

10/14/2020
5:45 p.m.
A trip of a lifetime that changed my lifetime. What was I thinking, ripping out a postcard from the back of an outdated magazine laying on the coffee table in Dante's Hair Salon and sending it away for information? That was such a big leap of faith to trust my life with a company I knew nothing about and to sign up for 12 days of daily hikes. One quick choice changed the trajectory of my life.

It is early fall in Bend, Oregon, and I am watching the bright sun set behind Mount Bachelor and the Cascade Mountains though my three-pane rectangular window and thinking of the other choices I have made that have also altered the direction of my life. There's been more than a handful in the last 22 years. Inadvertently, those choices were made while traveling or shortly after returning from a trip. Interesting!

Travel seems to do, for me, what nothing else does. Whether it's a weekend trip to Lake Shasta or San Francisco, a three-week cross-country road trip to see family, or a 45-minute brisk walk around the Deschutes River Trail, I am able to slow my mind down and see things more clearly within me and around me that

I'm not able to see as clearly or quickly when I am living my day-to-day life.

For this one reason, I'm so glad I decided 8 years ago to make it a habit to connect with my inner traveler – aka Zolfo Woman – daily. I love it when Zolfo Woman notices my heartbeat slowing down – mostly due to semi-conscious living. When that happens, she acts like a defibrillator sending a jolt to my heart. Magically, there is a sensation that causes an uptick in the rhythm of my Traveler's Heart. She really helps me to feel more connected and in sync with what matters most in my life, including everyone I'm blessed to have in it.

Another way I stay connected to my inner traveler is the only jewelry piece I wear on my right ring finger. I purchased this green stone ring in Queenstown, New Zealand on January 9, 1998. I instinctively knew then I wanted to take home the spirit of New Zealand and that traveler girl I unpacked.

The good vibes coming from this ring are real. It keeps me connected to that courageous girl who dared to leave home alone to discover she was more at home exploring the world, making soul-stirring connections and meaningful contributions in the world far beyond the four walls of a house.

Have you noticed that when you are part of a whole, you feel more connected and whole yourself? Every person – regardless of their sex, age, race, nationality, or status – has a fundamental need for connection. What I have learned traveling to six continents and speaking directly with people from all walks of life (verbally, with hand gestures, and with dirt drawings) is that we have a common yearning… to belong, to bond, to touch, to be close, and to feel part of something greater than ourselves. Sadly, it took a world pandemic and Covid-19 to expose our most vulnerable feelings of ache, insignificance, despair, and loneliness when real connection is restricted, denied, or temporarily abolished.

What I've come to appreciate over these last 8 months is that these Covid-19 times are similar to my extensive travel days. They both offer great teachings and even greater opportunities to reset the connections in my life. Whether at home or living on the road, I'm very clear that I am responsible for creating new ways to bond with my family and friends near and far. I want to be cooperative and compassionate with my neighbors and community. I know to embrace downtimes and to value what a gift extra time really is. And the biggest opportunity that Covid-19, along with traveling, gives me is to practice letting go of going it alone, so that others can support me, be there for me, and give to me.

So, while I may miss giving my dad a live hug, getting a phone call, and hearing his voice is that much more treasured right now. While I miss playing the game Connect 4 with my 5-year-old nephew sitting by the fireplace in Safeway as we enjoy our donuts, we were able to get creative with sticky notes and a black Sharpie. Now Jack and I play Connect 4 via zoom, AND he's learning his numbers that we taped over each of the seven columns. And while I miss going to Sunday service at Westside, I now spend alone time speaking with God on the pine-tree-lined hiking trails of Central Oregon... and not just on Sundays, anymore. I can honestly say I speak with Him more now than I ever did before, and I hear Him here more than in any church I've ever attended.

Crises, change, and travel have a way of inviting me to journey within. It is here, in the quiet and the stillness of my heart and soul, that the feeling of home is strongly experienced. It rises up to meet and greet me. It is here that I feel most safe, protected, loved, and even hugged. And it is here, in this moment and space, that I remember I'm never more than a heartbeat away from feeling connected with all that truly matters most and with my wise guide inside.

REFLECTION ON H: FINDING AN "IN" WHEN YOU ARE "OUT" IN THE WORLD

READ ANY TRAVEL article or blog, and you will see that making new connections with diverse people around the world is one of the top benefits of traveling. One of the fastest ways travelers connect is by simply taking an interest in the person they just met at a coffee shop, on the plane, walking on a trail, or while wandering down a cobblestone backstreet of a charming small town. By asking relatable, open-ended questions and offering undivided attention, an instant connection is often made. If you're fortunate, a quick bond is created which has the potential to be life changing and life lasting. Has that happened to you while traveling?

What if you took this "interest" approach when you returned home? Imagine what more you could learn about a person when you travel beyond the cliché question, "What do you do for a living?"

Here are a few of my favorite conversation starters. Pick one or two and try them out. By taking an interest in someone else, the only risk you run is that person taking the same interest in you. Would that be so bad?

- If you could live anywhere for a year, where would it be and why?
- Who is your favorite family member and why?
- What movie would you have liked to be the star of?
- If you could teach something, what would it be?
- What's the word "home" mean to you?
- Where would you like to travel next and why?
- What did you dream of being when you grew up?
- What skills have you learned through traveling that you can add to your resume?
- What is your favorite way to spend your birthday?
- What comforts you when you are having a bad day?
- What has travel prepared you for in life?
- When in your life have you laughed the hardest?
- Would you rather travel into space or to the depths of the ocean? Why?
- Tell me more about the one movie you can watch over and over again.
- What is your favorite season?
- If you could live in another time period, what would it be?
- What is the legacy story about yourself you never grow tired of telling?
- One a scale of one to ten - with ten the highest – how would you rate traveling alone?

- What is the most interesting thing you've learned or read recently?
- Whom in the world would you most like to share a meal with?
- What do people misunderstand about you? (Not a first question - but very telling!)
- What are five traits you value in your best friend?

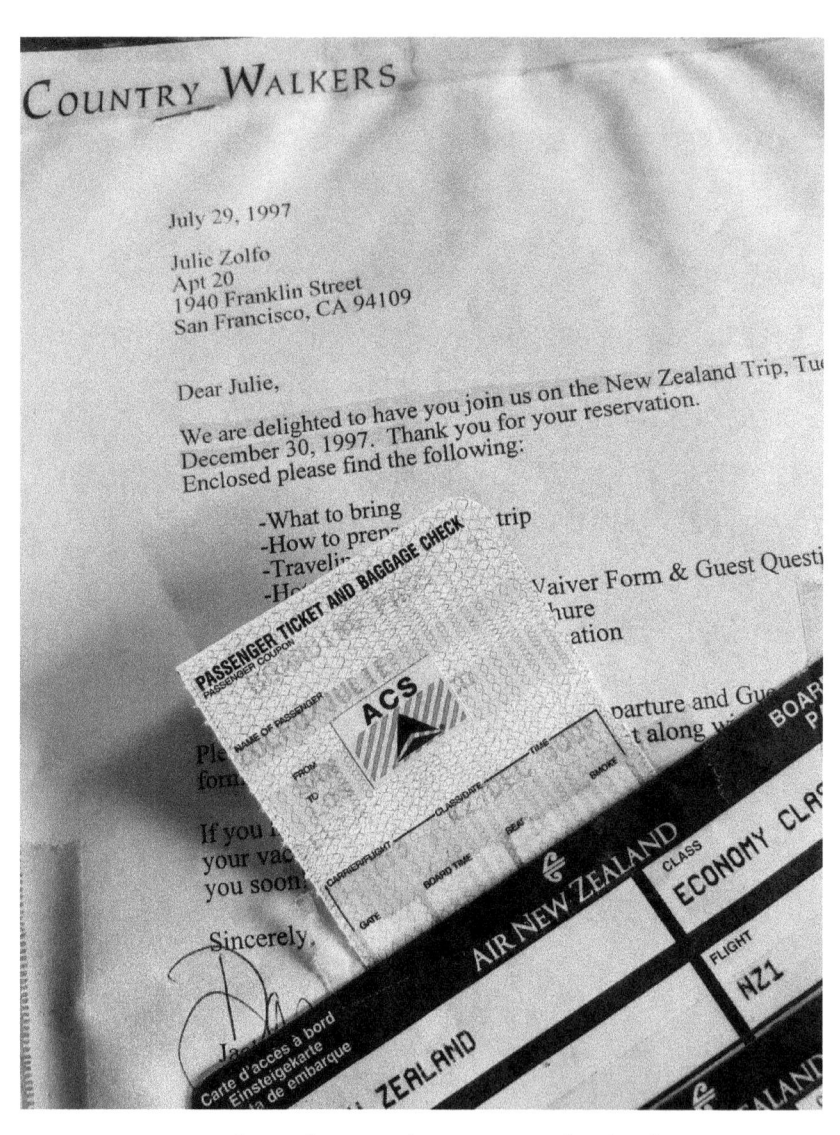

Welcome letter and Air New Zealand ticket

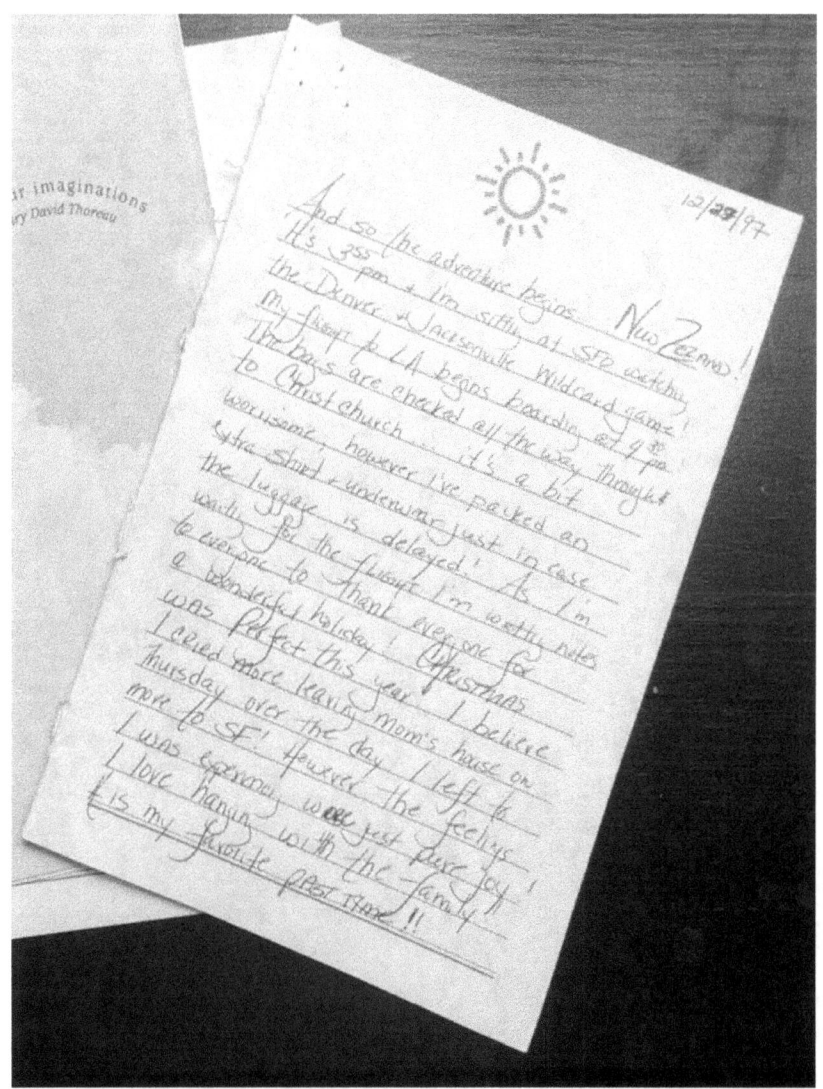

First page of my New Zealand Journal

All smiles with Guide Eddie, Cyd, and Carol

Lodge mementos and note from my sister

Day hikes and constellation map

WISDOM:
EXPERIENCE WITHOUT EXPECTATIONS

DESIRE:
CURIOSITY

IN 1999, I took a nine-month sabbatical from my job as the Director of Travel Industry Sales at PIER 39 in San Francisco to backpack solo through Bangkok * Northern Thailand * Burma * Laos * Bangkok * Nepal * Bangkok * Southern Thailand * Penang * Eastern Malaysia * Singapore * Italy * Greece * Cyclades Islands * Egypt * London * Whales * Liverpool * Ireland.

But it was the twenty-one-day trek in the Himalayas on the Annapurna Circuit that opened the door to the joys of living a life of curiosity. And it was during this spur-of-the-moment visit to Nepal that I mastered the art of experiencing life without expectations.

PART 1

You know that feeling you have when you find money in the pocket of a jacket you put away the previous winter? You feel lucky because it is found money, but it was already your money, so you feel a different satisfaction when you hold that money in your hand. That is how I felt when I was traveling for two weeks in New Zealand in January 1998. I felt so lucky, but I'd worked hard by planning and saving for the trip, so it was luck I had earned.

I wanted to feel that way again. It was the adventure. It was the travel. It was the curiosity. I knew that two weeks – the typical corporate vacation allotment – was not long enough. I became obsessed with traveling again.

I knew I had the tools to figure out how to make it happen. I had a bachelor's degree in business marketing. I was raised by, and worked for, a father who restructured major corporations to prepare them for liquidation. And I was the director of travel industry sales for PIER 39 in San Francisco. The tools I had to take on this project were preparedness, organization, research, and curiosity.

I created The Five Fundamentals of Planning a Trip:
1. Time
2. Destination
3. Money
4. People
5. Purpose

The first questions I ask myself are about time. When will I go? How long can I go for? And is there a particular time of year that is optimum for traveling to the destination?

The next questions, which are probably the most important, have to do with money. How much am I willing to spend? Do I have a limit? Do I have to save for this trip? What expenses can I anticipate, and what expenses might come up unexpectedly, such as surprise excursions?

The third set of questions is about destination. Is there a place that I've always wanted to visit? Are there parts of the world that I can overland easily? How am I going to get there? How will I travel once in the country?

Next are questions about people. Who will I travel with? I didn't really consider this factor for my trip in 1999. I knew that I wanted to travel and that I was ready to head out on my own. I did plan to meet fellow travelers along the way, but I did not have to consider other people and their expectations or limitations when planning my trip.

The final questions I consider when planning my trips revolve around purpose. Why am I going? (Usually, it's because I want that lucky feeling to continue.) And will the why affect the where?

With those questions in mind, I planned my next trip. I started with research: books, travel guides, magazines, and other people. People in my life had traveled, so I spoke to them about the places they found the most interesting. My dad and his friend had traveled to Southeast Asia, as had my coworker Matt, who had just returned to work after traveling for a year.

So, my focus became the Pacific Rim. It was inexpensive, which was a driving force when considering my budget. Also, it would be summer the whole time. With each question partially answered, I was better able to plan.

That is when I created "The Binder." I made color-coordinated tabs for each section, including:

- Places to go
- How to get there
- How to travel overland
- Holidays
- Weather
- Visa requirements
- Vaccinations
- CDC requirements
- Phrases and customs
- Religions of the region

During my planning stage, I inquired with my employer about a sabbatical. We were part of the travel industry. We believed in promoting travel. And PIER 39 believed that travel included their employees.

A friend was going to sublet my apartment, so that removed the worry of moving and/or storing my housewares and personal belongings.

Next, I worked on a budget. I had been saving for a car. It wasn't really something I needed in San Francisco. It would have been a nice luxury to have a car at my disposal, but not a necessity. So, I transferred car money to my travel savings.

My binder was filling up, and I thought I had answered every question at least three times. Then I sat with my father and realized that I didn't have anything figured out *at all!*

"What more do I need to consider?" I asked for both his business and travel opinions, which I respected because of his expertise and the fact that he was my dad.

"As your appointed power of attorney, I want to know how to handle your last wishes if you die on this trip. What should I do with your personal items such as your clothes, music CDs, financial investments, and jewelry, if you die during this adventure of yours?"

"Ummm..."

"Do you have a will?"

"A will?"

"What songs and readings would you like at your wake? Do you have funeral arrangements outlined?"

"Did you really just ask what song to play at my funeral?" I had not expected this line of questioning.

"Yes. Do you have a plan?"

"Wow!" I laughed. "You killed me and my confidence in the first three minutes of conversation."

My dad had taken a similar trip to Southeast Asia a few years prior. "Mr. Routine, Structure, and All Things First Class" spent several weeks backpacking through North Thailand and Borneo with his friend Denis. I knew he was supportive of my adventure. But his practical thinking and notorious bluntness caught me off guard. I did come to him for advice, and the questions he posed were important, so I considered each one. Over the course of the few weeks before my trip, I answered them.

After the talk with my dad, I set up an after-work meeting with my coworker and friend, Matt. I wanted to go over all of my research.

We sat at the restaurant with my binder in front of me, complete with its bright, shiny tabs and indexes. The pages were stuffed with information such as "kiss, bow, and shake hands." There wasn't anything I wanted to forget or miss.

Matt smiled and listened. My voice rose in excitement as I went through the binder and asked him questions. Finally, I finished showing him my prized possession, so proud of my organizational skills.

"How much does that weigh? Are you going to carry that around in your backpack the whole trip?"

His implications were clear. The binder was heavy and large. Ironically, it contained information about how much you should pack and how heavy to make your load. My "Aha!" moment became an "ARGH!" moment. I knew he was right.

Looking back, I don't feel foolish for making the binder. I needed to do the research. It was important to answer my five fundamentals and have the information to back up each finding. Even though I was figuratively throwing out the binder and traveling without reservations or set plans, I still had a foundation. And the research was all part of the curiosity. I found all the information I needed to get started, but I was going to travel without expectations and allow for the experience.

PART 2

"Is this the bus to Pokhara?" As the sentence left my lips, I was instantly transported 7,500 miles around the globe from Nepal to a former, more insulated, and less adventurous life. I was a teenager again, sitting with my younger brother on my family's green sectional couch in our New Jersey home. We were watching *Romancing the Stone*. I cringed with embarrassment as Joan Wilder – an untraveled, mousey, New-York-City-dwelling romance novelist – poorly navigated her way through South America while frantically trying to save her kidnapped sister Elaine.

Fifteen years later, I was the awkward outsider standing in my colorful patchwork hoodie with my oversized AcrTeryx Bora 62 backpack on the chaotic streets of Durbar Square in Kathmandu. I inhaled the cross-pollination of exhaust fumes, turmeric spices, and cow poop, uncertain where to catch the next bus to Pokhara.

I'd asked the petite, brown, weathered woman standing next to me. Her face bore the deep, etched lines of hardship. A wine-barrel-sized straw basket was strapped to her back. She graciously answered my inquiry by pointing.

I turned in the indicated direction and spotted a dilapidated school bus parked about a hundred yards ahead, already overflowing with locals, backpackers, and a variety of livestock. I thanked her with a smile and a slight bow.

As I zig-zagged through the rickshaws and bicycles, I skirted young children playing in water that streamed from a pipe. The elderly bathed in it and young women washed dishes and clothes. I also passed a pungent, flesh-smelling butcher shop. One goat was tied to a stake while another lay slain in the dirt road, hoofs up and ready to be sold. My shaky inner voice whispered to me, "Are you ready for this, Julie?"

Yards from the bus, I felt a heaviness on my chest which I assumed was from the front-load-lifter straps on my backpack. Ironically, loosening the straps only made my heartbeat faster, causing sweat to seep through and soak my sweatshirt.

This was not a normal feeling for me, but then my normal was changing daily, sometimes moment by moment. I took a deep breath and exhaled. I took another deep breath and exhaled again. After the third deep breath, I did what I did best in these rare moments – I recited an incantation for my safety and sanity prior to boarding the overcrowded death-trap I was voluntarily boarding to Pokhara:

You are Zolfo Woman.
You are fearless and courageous in all you do.
You are joyfully curious about everything and everyone.
You have unwavering faith in God,
even in crazy, shit-scary moments.
You are Zolfo Woman.

How did I get here?

Until two years earlier, I'd played it safe and didn't know the true feeling of adventure through travel. That feeling started when I was trekking through New Zealand with a group of close strangers and looking up at the stars. The stars had never looked brighter. My breath and spirit had never felt more certain. I was happier and more satisfied with the ground beneath my feet, the mountains surrounding me, and the world before me. I knew something had changed, but I wasn't sure what. I just knew that I wanted more. When I returned home, I started making plans to travel the world.

So, in January 1999, I set out on train, plane, bus, ferry, boat, and feet to travel the world. I landed in Bangkok, Thailand on January 26. Before leaving home, I had planned a trip overland through Southeast Asia because friends and family had successfully done the route and told me of the beautiful cities and beaches and jungles and mountains. I'd planned nothing other than my starting point. I would let one moment take me to the next.

Along the way, I met other travelers who shared a mindset of immersing ourselves in the place and culture. We often traveled together for a day or two, then parted ways to either continue toward our respective destinations or to change course and follow in the footsteps of a fellow traveler, going where they'd just been.

I traveled by bus and pickup trucks through northern Thailand into Burma, hopped on a speedboat on the Mekong River heading east into Laos, and visited Luang Prabang and Wein Wien in Laos.

As I walked through the dirt streets of Luang Prabang, I happened across a few Brits who were looking for travelers to fill their boat to visit the caves. As I had been doing with my travels so far, I said, "Why not?"

Eileen, Barry, and Stephen were very nice. The boat ride was nice. The caves were boring. But I was glad I went because they shared their experience of Nepal and trekking the Annapurna Circuit in the Himalayas.

They told me I had to go there. They described the villages and mountains. They described the peace.

Our discussion piqued my curiosity.

"Of course, you are going to Nepal," one of them said when I told them it wasn't on my mental list of countries to visit. I didn't even know that part of the world existed until I got there. Traveling through Southeast Asia was like coming to a fork in the road. Each time I came to a new fork, I had the freedom to decide which way to go. And when I met Eileen, Barry, and Stephen for dinner that night, Nepal was all I could think about. Their stories, told over rounds of beer, inspired my decision: the Annapurna trek was the next adventure I would experience. We celebrated with a round of high fives and a few more rounds of beer.

Once again, as I had been doing in the six weeks since starting my adventure, I adjusted the plan I'd outlined in my forty-pound trip binder. I learned to listen to other travelers and my intuition. And that is how I found myself on my way to Pokhara to trek the legendary Himalayas, the greatest mountains in the world. I considered this new part of the trip to be extra special. Something solely for me – a very spiritual journey. I felt overwhelmed and grateful.

As described by guidebooks and countless fellow travelers, Pokhara promised to be a completely different feel and landscape from the hubbub of Kathmandu. It evoked images of snow-capped mountains, time-worn temples, laid-back town charm, and the best walking trails on earth.

As we unloaded onto the streets of the town center that night, we entered what appeared to be a dust bowl swirling in the air. The poor visibility made navigating an unfamiliar place more challenging. Thankfully, destiny was on my side that evening and led me straight to Hotel Monastery, which advertised hot water available daily, lemon tea, and amazing mountain views.

Since leaving San Francisco six weeks earlier, I had not stayed in a guesthouse or hotel for more than two consecutive nights. For the next three nights, I had my own clean-yet-sparse room with a single wooden-frame bed and a private bathroom with a shower that had hot running water... all day.

OMG, a shower! Just the thought of hot water on my traveler's body brought bliss to my heart. If this was roughing it, I was all in... all for a cool $7 a night.

Once in bed, I closed my eyes to replay this wonderful day in my mind's eye. Little did I know when I started my day in Kathmandu, a bit frazzled, that I would feel so at peace and grateful by the day's end. I drifted off to sleep, hoping the night would pass quickly in anticipation of seeing where I was... in the daylight!

During the night, a torrential rainstorm moved through the Pokhara Valley, taking with it the sepia-soaked air and pungent smells. What it left behind the next morning was something I had only seen in magazines and movies – blue skies and the snow-capped Himalaya Mountains. I don't think you have seen a mountain until you have seen the Himalayas.

But before I could get up close and personal with the heavenly mountain range, I had to figure out one minor detail. How does one go about trekking the Annapurna Circuit? Unlike other travelers who arrived in Pokhara to hike 120-140 miles of Himalayan terrain and summit over 17,000 feet, I was not well informed (or in trekking shape).

I could not sit at breakfast and look at the beautiful mountains for long if I wanted to climb them. It was time to focus... My morning mission was to accomplish three things: get a trekking permit, hire a guide, and purchase winter clothes. Up to that point, my traveling wardrobe consisted of colorful imprinted sarongs, tank tops, bathing suits, and flip-flops. It was time to prepare for a colder experience.

I strolled down the twisted dirt road to the town center in search of some answers from the multitude of trekking shops. In the first shop, an American owner from Bozeman, Montana greeted me. He was helpful in answering my questions, but he only offered group treks of twenty or more Westerners. Before arriving in Nepal, I'd decided that I wanted a single excursion. Just me and a guide. I had traveled mostly on my own – meeting people here and there to share rides, meals, or rooms. After my two weeks in New Zealand with a group of strangers, I was interested in doing this one on my own.

In the second shop, an extraverted young Nepalese man cornered me into a wall of sleeping bags and told me why he would be the perfect porter. There was something too familiar about him. I wanted a guide, not a travel companion.

Like Goldilocks, I was feeling very unsatisfied at the lack of progress I was making on this mission. I entered the third store, Fair Mount Trekking Shop. Then something changed…

In this store, I was greeted with hot lemon tea from a smiling old man about half my height. In jumbled English, he asked my name and where I was from. I was so touched by his effort to connect using my language. I couldn't walk away. And he knew it.

The kind old man politely took me by the arm and led me to the back of the shop while he continued to ask about my plans in Pokhara. He invited me to sit, pointing to a pile of carpets against the wall. Was this true Nepalese hospitality or the best salesman I had encountered? I decided to play along.

The carpets I sat on while sipping my hot lemon tea were divine. Made from woven wool and silk, the carpets were embedded with images of the Himalayan Mountain range. I stood and looked down at the carpets. I felt the spirit of the mountains calling.

Sensing my fascination with the carpets and my lowered defenses (thanks to the hot lemon tea and hospitality), the old man seized the moment.

"You can see how these carpets are made when you choose our homestay trek option." (Of course, I can.)

The old man waved over a young Nepalese man who worked in the shop. "Julie, this is Bishnu. He is one of the best guides in all of Pokhara." If you agree today, our store will equip you with all your needs for a two-to-three-week Annapurna Circuit trek and provide Bishnu as your personal guide every step of the way. There is no other guide in the area I would trust to take a single woman."

Immediately, I gave Bishnu another scan. He wore an old blue-and-white T-shirt that appeared glued to his toned chest and lean, youthful frame. He paired the shirt with plaid gray, blue, and tan Bermuda-length shorts. Under his black baseball cap was tucked thick black hair which matched his dark, almond-shaped, bashful eyes. But what caught my eye was the expensive looking gold watch on his left wrist.

"Nice watch." I hoped to engage in a dialogue to hear the level of Bishnu's English, and of course to get the back-story on the jewelry piece.

"Thank you. It was a gift." Bishnu's English was good enough to understand, but probably not good enough that he would want to talk for hours and hours, day after day. I was here to find some inner peace and felt that would require some quiet time.

In less than a heartbeat, I knew Bishnu was the right guide to join me on the next part of my amazing adventure, which began before I even set foot on the mountain.

The day before we left, I anxiously prepared for an adventure I knew little to nothing about. I spent the afternoon determined to pack lighter than I already had. I dumped the contents of my backpack onto the floor of my hotel room and created three distinct piles.

The easiest pile to form was the store-for-later pile. Surely, I would not wear the two boho-hippie spaghetti-strapped sundresses I had worn interchangeably every day for six weeks before arriving in Pokhara. I was also confident I wouldn't need my one and only pair of dressy shoes. Those items would stay at the hotel until I got back.

The next two piles weren't as effortless to discern.

Most expert travel advice for efficient packing says that 99% of everywhere you go will have 99% of what you need, anywhere in the world. With that logic, it's best to pack half of what you think you need. I wasn't sure if that reasoning applied to a three-week trek in the Himalayas.

Looking at the two remaining piles, I knew where I had to scale back. Once I'd finalized the final-cut pile, I separated those items into even smaller groups and placed them in individual plastic bags I had collected and saved. This technique would help section items within the large backpack – a tip I learned from some fellow travelers back in North Thailand.

Three pairs of socks, three bras, and three underwear were placed in one bag, while three pants and three T-shirts went into another. I had a separate bag for toiletries and another one for winter clothes such as gloves, hat, and thermals. Miscellaneous items would be stuffed, last minute, in the top portion of the pack. My sleeping bag, jacket, and cleats, which I wouldn't need until I neared the summit nine or ten days into the trek, lined the bottom of the backpack.

I repeated the process of elimination for my day pack. Remembering the mantra "Less is more," I only considered critical-carry items. Sunscreen, first-aid supplies, some snacks, playing cards, a flashlight, a journal, a camera, a small tripod, and twelve rolls of film made the cut. Feeling very satisfied with my accomplishments, it was time for one last dinner in Pokhara.

I left the bags on the floor. I would check and recheck everything one last time in the morning before I joined Bishnu. But at the moment, I felt good.

When I returned to my room after dinner, I realized the door was unlocked. Did I forget to lock it? I placed my left hand into the pocket of my pants, pulled out my mace, and said anxiously, "Hello, is someone here?"

Silence.

I waited a few moments behind the slightly opened door before repeating myself. My tone became a bit more forceful, my adrenalin a lot more amped. Do I run or charge in? This sucks.

Forcefully, I swung the door open to have a complete view of the room. I pushed the door so hard it banged against the inside wall and rebounded just as quickly. With all my senses heightened, I thrust my right hand upward to stop the door from slamming back on me.

Once inside the room, my brain went into overdrive as I assessed the situation. At first glance, nothing looked disturbed. My bags appeared untouched. That was a relief. I looked at the nightstand and noticed my travel alarm, flashlight, and coins were unmoved. I exhaled a sigh of relief. It seemed the only thing disturbed in the room was me.

I walked my shaky Jell-O legs toward the single framed bed and sat on the edge, facing my bags. I was frozen, sitting in silence, staring into space. Thankfully, the stillness slowed down my heartbeat and allowed the white spots flashing before me to fade away.

Once I gained composure, I lay on my back and stared at the white ceiling above me. I replayed in my mind the events between when I left the room and when I returned.

Suddenly, I had a sick feeling. On my nightstand I also had a book, *Touching the Void*. Inside the book, I had placed the trekking permit and the money I planned to take on the trek. My adrenalin spiked again.

Oh crap!

Every day until then, I'd kept all my important papers and money on me at all times. Every traveler knows to do this. In my organizing process, I'd temporarily placed the trekking permit and money in the book. Why?

After dinner, I was going to condense all the items I was leaving behind. I didn't want to forget these two important items. I knew I would not forget the book, so this was my brilliant fail-safe idea. Now it didn't feel so brilliant or fail-safe.

In a panic, I jumped up and grabbed the book from the nightstand. I fumbled through the pages while praying, "St. Anthony, St. Anthony, please come around. Something is lost and it must be found."

If there was ever a time when I needed divine intervention, it was then.

A hearty, reverent "Yes!" left my lips when I found the trekking permit around page seventy. I seized the spine of the book and shook it vehemently. Within seconds, it started raining rupees on my bed.

I dropped to my knees in praise and thanks.

After lifting my humbled self from the floor, I prepared for bed. The next day would start very early, and I still needed to do the final packing.

As I undressed, I had an internal chat with myself. "So, Julie. I guess this proves you were at fault. Apparently, you forgot to lock the door before leaving for dinner. Thankfully, it all worked in your favor."

Travel always provides lessons. Unfortunately, some are learned through tough experiences on what *not* to do next time. In the future, I'd need to double check locking the door. More importantly, I needed to keep all important things *on me* at all times. That's Traveler Basic 101.

Falling asleep on that final night in Pokhara was easier knowing I'd simply made a mistake. It's challenging enough being a single woman traveling alone. I didn't need to pile on unwarranted fears or accusations. It was over and done with, no harm, no foul – just a good story to laugh at later.

The next morning, my alarm went off at 4:30 a.m. I still had to check and recheck the smaller bags before placing them in my large green pack. I still needed to check out of the room and place that the items I wasn't taking on my trek in storage. My final task was to assemble my daypack.

By 5:30 a.m., I'd finished those tasks. Sitting in the front lobby of the Hotel Monastery, I arranged my day pack to ensure my critical-carry items were easily accessible throughout the day.

Inside the bag, I had a few first-aid items such as band-aids, first-aid cream, ibuprofen, duct tape, and a bungee rope; these were all placed at the bottom of the bag. Layered on top of that group was an extra pair of socks, an extra set of shoelaces, sunscreen, and lip balm.

I clipped my water bottle to the front of my pack. That left four items to load: snacks, my journal, my camera, and twelve rolls of film. One by one, I placed those items into my red day pack.

Snacks, check.

Journal, check.

Film, check.

Camera... Where was the camera?

I had it the day before during the pile separation process. I knew this because I removed the roll of film that was in the camera and placed it in the store-for-later pile. I wanted to start the trek with a fresh roll of film. Perhaps I'd accidentally placed my camera in storage.

Knowing Bishnu would arrive in less than fifteen minutes, I rushed back to the storage area. I opened the locker and rummaged through my clothes, jewelry, shoes, souvenirs, and extra rolls of film. No camera.

I told myself to slow down and look again. It had to be there.

I decided the best thing to do was to remove each item to confirm the camera wasn't tangled among my softer items, like the sarongs and sundresses. One by one, I removed shoes, rolls of film, bathing suits, sundresses, and sarongs. Only a small plastic bag of jewelry remained in the locker.

What the heck is going on here? Where is my camera?

I put everything back in the locker, relocked it, rechecked that it was locked, and rushed back to the lobby. Thoughts of the previous night's unlocked door haunted me.

Wheezing, I greeted Bishnu with a half-hearted hello. Before he could say anything, I told him about my camera dilemma. I had looked everywhere except in the perfectly packed large backpack which leaned against the wall nearby.

With despair, I brought the backpack into the sitting area and did what I needed to do. I unbuckled the bag, flipped it upside down, and shook it fiercely. The smaller bags crashed onto the floor.

Once the entire pack was empty, I sat on the floor and picked through each bag, praying silently that the camera somehow got misplaced during my packing. Would I be so blessed as to receive a second miracle from St. Anthony in less than twenty-four hours?

When I realized there were no more bags to look through, my heart sank into the floor. It was like I was anchored and couldn't move. I noticed an audience of onlookers – including my guide, the hotel manager, and a few trekkers – standing at a distance. No one said a word, but I could read the pity on their faces. I broke the silence.

"We'll leave in a few minutes to trek one of the most scenic and legendary places on this planet, and I don't have a camera. Got twelve rolls of film, but my camera has gone missing. This looks as sucky to you as it feels for me."

Fighting back tears, I re-stuffed the smaller bags into the backpack. Bishnu walked closer and helped me repack. He tried to comfort me with a smile, but I couldn't reciprocate.

I had carefully planned the number of pictures I was going to allot myself for each day, thinking about how I needed to capture each moment and the scenery before me. The pictures would also prove to the world that my trip actually happened. Would people believe me without the photos? Would I remember the trip when I got home if I did not have pictures to back up each memory?

It felt like a setback, and I allowed myself to be mad. It's not an emotion I liked to express, but at that moment, being upset would not help the situation. I needed some clarity and courage to pull me through this more than I needed compassion.

Once I repacked the bag, I walked over to the hotel manager. I shared the story of my room door being open when I returned from dinner the night before. I thought he should be aware of the possibility that an unauthorized person may have entered my room and taken the camera. I had no proof other than knowing I had the camera the day before.

With my newly repacked bags, Bishnu and I finally got on our way, thirty minutes later than expected. To make up time, we took a cab to get to the bus. About ten minutes into the ride, Bishnu and the taxi driver spoke intensely, as if they were getting into an argument. No more drama, Universe. Please.

After a few minutes of silence, the taxi driver stopped in front of a store. The sign on the door said it was closed, but the driver banged on the door anyway. No one answered. He banged again. No answer.

The driver looked back at Bishnu, who gave the driver a look in return. The driver pounded one more time. This time, the door opened. Standing there was a middle-aged man wearing only pants and smoking a cigarette.

Bishnu turned to me and said, "Today Sunday. No stores open. Here you can buy a camera. Maybe little more. Go look?"

Wow! I didn't see that coming. The language barrier never interfered with Bishnu's understanding of my distress over my camera situation. He went out of his way to help me, even when I didn't respond to his help at the hotel. I felt like the Grinch whose heart grew three sizes in one day because a stranger was nice to me, even when I wasn't nice to him.

I didn't let the start of my morning hamper the day. Once we got off the bus at the beginning of the trail, we set out on foot, walking for an hour and a half before coming to the village of Karputar. This was the first of many nights that I would get to a village and have to look for a place to eat and sleep. I quickly learned to reign in my expectations. For 100R, ($1.50) I had a bed, a room, and a hole in the dirt floor for a toilet.

What a first day on the trail! I got to ride in a bus with goats, women, and children. I looked out at the clear blue sky and saw my first real glimpse of the Himalayas. And I got to live among the Nepalese. Children were everywhere, covered in dirt and dust and shooting each other with water guns. The people were friendly, always saying "Namaste" and "Hello," followed by "Where are you from?" They had no inhibitions about speaking with Westerners. This was the immersion experience I was looking for.

On day two, I asked Bishnu how the day would compare to the first one. His answer was, "Same, same."

He lied! By 11:30 a.m., we had navigated a wobbly suspension bridge (Go, Zolfo Woman!) and crossed the river about a dozen times. We walked over a million rocks as we made our way along the riverbank. We didn't do any of that on the first day.

But also, on my second day on the trek, I noticed something important. I was acclimating myself to a new world of sounds. This world had roosters, goats, cows, chickens, birds, foreign voices, and at times even silence. I had profound thoughts about silence and the power that comes with it. I had always liked the outdoors, but I was learning to really hear nature.

Maybe this is what the British travelers meant when they were talking about peace. It is more than the peace you feel when you're alone; it's that next step of shutting out your own mind's chatter and just listening. Silence can be very loud.

On each of the next few days, we walked approximately four and a half hours across rocky terrain, going uphill. We ended our days around 1:30 p.m. to eat lunch, take a nap, and play rummy 500. Bishnu was getting the hang of the game, and we could play for three hours without even looking up.

Before we left Pokhara, Bishnu had learned that the Thorung La Pass was closed because of a storm, and people were having to turn back before the summit. It was still closed, and I kept praying, "Please. Please. Please God… I've come all this way! Please let me pass!"

On day five, we extended our days by thirty minutes. The five hours uphill was making me stronger.

Also on day five, I dove deeper into my immersion experience. Deeper into my experience without expectation. It was time to wash my clothes in a rushing river. And Bishnu was going to teach me how.

Prior to the trek, there wasn't much washing to do. In Thailand, I lived in my bathing suits and sarongs. All I had to do was rinse them in a bathroom sink and hang them to dry. When I needed to clean more personal items, I cleaned the sink with one of my handy baby wipes and then clogged the drain with something. Next, I used water from the sink if it had a faucet, or I collected shower water in my water bottle and then dumped it into the sink. The water from both sources often looked dirtier than the clothes I needed to wash. I chose to be less stinky over less clean.

If I got really lazy, I would buy new clothes since they were so inexpensive. If I got bored with my clothes, I would trade them with another traveler or simply leave them behind in my room, hoping the right person would come along who would appreciate the unexpected gift.

It was time for more adventurous cleaning methods.

I stuffed two stretchy pairs of hiking socks, two cool-dry T-shirts, one pair of convertible traveler's pants, three undies, a small towel, and sleeping shorts into a crumpled gray plastic bag I had in my daypack. Next, I found the biodegradable green liquid camping soap in the supply section of my backpack. I felt very proud that I was so prepared.

Then I walked from my room, down a narrow, dark hall which dumped me into the small, musty check-in area of the lodge. There, I found Bishnu. He was sitting on a wooden bench with some other Nepalese guides.

To my surprise, Bishnu was wearing a different blue T-shirt for the first time on the trek. It took me a moment to adjust to the change. Laying across his legs was his infamous blue-and-white, T-shirt and one pair of socks. How typical.

I concluded that some stereotypical behaviors are gender specific, not just cultural. My pride bubble burst when I realized the four-to-one ratio of a woman's wash pile to a man's. Chuckling under my breath, I said, "Where to, Bishnu?"

"I know the perfect place little-little down the road." I'd heard that sentence one too many times. Bishnu knew what was on the line – wash before rummy – so it was up to him to help make this process quick and easy.

We walked in the same direction I had just returned from thirty minutes prior. Before reaching the center of town again, Bishnu veered right. He directed me to walk down a short but steep gravel-and-dirt path which appeared to lead us away from any sort of structured washroom or common wash area with an accessible water source. Where was he taking me?

I was looking down, focused on my feet and the uneven ground. I didn't have my walking sticks to help stabilize my body. To make matters worse,

I was wearing flip-flops. I had not planned to go on a mini excursion to complete my washing.

Each time I placed my foot in front of me, it slid a few inches before it stopped. My legs shook and my mind raced. I hadn't come this far to slip on loose rocks, fall backwards, split my head open on something pointy, and have to be air-lifted out of the Himalayas. My story would have a better ending.

I was concentrating so hard on not falling that I blocked out everything else happening around me. By the time I looked up, I realized Bishnu had kept his promise and brought me to a water source.

Like a gazelle, Bishnu swiftly and gracefully hopped over the large boulders, took off his sandals, and stood in water up to his calves. He waved me over to join him.

Whatever the opposite of a gazelle is, that was me. I cautiously walked across the rocks, holding my arms out to balance myself. Seeing my struggles, Bishnu shouted for me to toss my plastic clothes bag toward him, so I had no distractions. By this time, he was having a good laugh at me.

I finally arrived at the edge of the riverbank and joined Bishnu in the water. I hadn't thought about the temperature of the water until my feet were submerged. Immediately, I broke into song. "Oh shit, oh fuck, oh shit, oh fuck!"

After the shock wore off and my feet became numb, I asked Bishnu what to do next. "Watch me," he said with a big grin.

Bishnu submerged his favorite blue-and-white T-shirt into the river. After the pre-wash cycle, he spread the shirt across a smooth rock. Next, he reached into the side pocket of his shorts and removed a small rectangular bar of soap – the type that hotels give their guest for free. Now it was time for the wash cycle.

Bishnu placed the bar of soap directly onto the T-shirt and scrubbed and scrubbed and scrubbed. He didn't miss a square inch. Once the T-shirt was completely covered with suds, Bishnu submerged it into the river again to remove all the soap. Next came the spin cycle – or, as we called it at the river, the slam cycle.

In one motion, Bishnu removed the T-shirt from under the water, flipped it over his right shoulder and then slammed the shirt against a rock in front of him. (This process helps remove any remaining dirt quickly and dislodges excess water.) After a half-dozen slams, Bishnu laid the T-shirt on a clean, flat rock to dry under the afternoon rays of the sun.

"Now you go." He pointed to me.

Over the next thirty minutes, Bishnu and I washed our clothes silently, in tandem. It was almost like a scene from the movie "A River Runs Through it," only we were in the Himalayas, not Montana, and we were washing clothes by hand, not fly-fishing. And I was with a Nepalese guide named Bishnu, not with a smoking-hot actor named Brad Pitt. Like I said, almost!

After we washed the clothes, we needed to wait for them to dry. Thankfully, the sun was still shining and had some warmth to it. This seemed to be the perfect opportunity to relax. I wanted to take a nap. Bishnu had another plan.

Reaching into the other side pocket of his shorts, Bishnu pulled out my deck of playing cards and asked with puppy dog eyes, "Can we play rummy now?"

On the first night of our trek, from the moment I laid the playing cards on the table and explained the rules of the game, Bishnu was hooked – a borderline addict in the making. He couldn't play enough rounds.

Interestingly, a new side of his personality revealed itself once the cards were shuffled. My quiet, mild-mannered Nepalese companion, whose patience and gentleness I leaned on throughout this trek, fell to the wayside. Sitting across from me now was my competitor, a more aggressive, spirited individual seeking to win bragging rights at all costs. Just how many rummy games our new relationship could handle would be tested.

With our clean clothes drying on the rock, I said, "I don't have my journal on me right now. How are we going to keep score?" I had been using the back pages of my travel journal to record each hand we played. To date, we were halfway through our first game of rummy 5000 instead of Rummy 500 (I had created a monster) and I was ahead by 200 points. I wasn't willing to play if we couldn't add our scores to the current tallies.

Just when I thought I had side-stepped the landmine to play, Bishnu reached back into the same side pocket where he pulled out the bar of soap. Like a magician doing his next trick, he produced a napkin and pencil. The game was on.

When we arrived back at the guesthouse, we learned what to expect over the next few days. We were about four days from Manang, where we would stay two extra days to acclimate to the altitude. The pass would hopefully open in five to seven days, which meant we were going to be fine. I also learned that we would walk in waist-deep snow for about three and a half hours. Maybe some planning – and not just taking the fork in the road with no research – would have been helpful after all...

Days six, seven, and eight brought more of the same. Each morning as he poured over the maps, I asked Bishnu what our day was going to be like. His answer was the same as he'd given on day two: "Same, same."

Day nine was a little different. The night before, we had met about a dozen travelers who were talking about crossing the summit in five days. It was raining, and they feared that there would be snow on the pass. I wasn't sure if that meant the trek would merely be harder, or if we'd have to stop. But I knew that we had a five-day journey to the pass, and then it would take seven days to descend the mountain. I was counting the days for my trek to be over. The Himalayas were possibly a once-in-a-lifetime chance, and I was growing and experiencing every moment. And each day, I was proud of what I did. But it was really hard, mentally, and physically.

On day nine, I climbed the Upper Pisang trail to 12,041 ft and came face to face with Annapurna II (26,040 ft), Lamjung Himai (22,740 ft), Annapurna III (24,787 ft), and Gangapurna (24,459 ft), stretching out before me. The view was truly awesome! None of the travelers from the night before reached that elevation. When we got back to camp, they told me they old trekked the Lower Pisang trail. The Upper Pisang kicked me in the butt, but I am so proud that I did it.

It showed me that I beat myself up a little to accomplish things. My boss at PIER 39, Denise, always told me that my expectations of myself were high. As I thought about Denise, I pulled out my St. Christopher medal my coworkers at PIER 39 gave me as a going-away gift. I rubbed the medal and said, "Yes. Yes, they are."

But without those high expectations to push myself, I wouldn't be able to expand my horizons. Look at what I got from it.

On day nine, we finally reached Manang, where we needed to stay for two nights to acclimate to the altitude of 11,614 ft before moving to a higher altitude. The saying is "Climb high. Sleep low." At the pace we were going, we would cross the pass on my grandfather's 90th birthday, March 12.

On day ten, I attended a briefing with the Himalaya Medical Rescue Service Association. The lecture was on AMS (Acute Mountain Sickness), which is very serious when the elevation is 17,769 ft (For comparison, the elevation of High Point, New Jersey is 1,803 ft; San Francisco, California is 52 ft). They recommended ascending 300 meters daily. On actual pass day, the climb would be 1000 meters. We would leave at daybreak to arrive at noon, because it takes another four to five hours to descend.

On day eleven, we finally set out on the trail from Manang to Yak Kharka, which was 12,800 ft. All uphill. When we arrived in Yak Kharka, I had breathing difficulties and a pounding headache. I was very worried because those are typical signs of AMS. I ate, took Dialox, and slept for three hours, which seemed to do the trick.

I woke up from that nap and immediately thought again, "How did I get here?" When I met those Brits and declared, "Himalayas? Nepal? I'm in!" I hadn't anticipated what "I'm in" fully meant. The wind gusted through the stone walls of my little room. I huddled under two extra blankets and my down sleeping bag – while wearing all of my clothes – and I was still freezing! I was overwhelmed by the enormity of it all. But then I remembered, with only 5,000 ft left to reach the summit, this was just an experience without the planned expectations, and I was on an amazing journey. Not just a journey through the tallest mountains in the world. A journey through the biggest part of me.

On day twelve, we reached 14,600 ft and arrived in Phedi. This was the last village before the crossing. It was on that day I realized I might have been a little crazy for doing this. The path was very steep and covered with ice and snow. It was one foot in front of the other. I felt that I'd had enough adventure to last me the rest of my life. Many times, I was ready to yell, "This is it! I am going to die!"

Day thirteen was on March 12, 1999. My grandfather's 90th birthday. We both accomplished great feats that day. He summited ninety decades on this earth. I summited 17,769 ft and stood on the top of the world!

Here are the actual words from my journal.

Date: 3/12/99 – Day #13
Location: Bob Marley Hotel, Mukinath, Nepal
Companions: Bishnu, Jackie (UK)
Day's Events: BIG DAY – CROSSED THORUNG LA

First and Foremost… I DID IT!
It was a hell of a day that started at 4:00 a.m.! With a full set of stars in the sky and the ¼ moon glowing, it was off to breakfast at 4:30 a.m. I convinced Bishnu that I didn't feel comfortable leaving at 4:00 a.m., so I got him to agree to 5:30 a.m. So, with flashlights in hand and fully armored in long underwear, sweatpants, sweatshirts, a down coat, a scarf, gloves, and gators, we were off to begin the biggest day of the trek!

The first ½ we ascended to 16,781 ft – it was literally straight up! Thank God I did most of it in the dark, so I never really saw how steep it was. After another 3 ½ hours (never ending hours) of false summits, we arrived at Thorung La at 10:30 a.m. – having climbed to 17,769 ft! The emotions I was feeling were so intense – I was scared and feared I wouldn't make it at some points. Then I was motivated and inspired seeing the prayer flags from a distance. Upon the arrival at base, I cried! There was so much pressure building up over the last five days – it was no longer a fun trek but a mission to cross Thorung La – it was so intense – every night people would sit with their trekking guides and maps and figure out their course for the next day. I began to hate the trek – it wasn't fun anymore – but once I got to the top, all the fears, anxieties, and doubts were placed to rest…I DID IT!

Seven days later, Bishnu and I were on an open-air bus back into Pokhara. Soon we would part ways. I wasn't prepared to say goodbye, so I created a diversion during the chaos of unloading the van.

"Bishnu, I'm tired now. Let's meet for lunch tomorrow and one more game of rummy."

He smiled in answer.

By 9:55 p.m., I was back at Monastery Lodge – the place it all started. I hadn't stayed up that late in three weeks. I was trying to acclimate to life in lower altitudes among crowds, so I stayed at the restaurant to watch the featured daily movie *Shakespeare in Love*.

Was it all a dream? The last three weeks were the most challenging, most enlightening, most thrilling. My eyes were opened to a world not my own. To be surrounded by incredible beauty daily while delving into cultures I had only read about transformed my heart.

The next day, Bishnu arrived freshly showered, shaven, and not wearing his blue-and-white T-shirt. After a long exchange of smiles, I held up the deck of cards and asked, "Are you ready to lose one more time?"

He replied, "I'm winning!" He grinned broadly while pointing his thumbs back at himself.

Before starting our final game, I recommended we order lunch from the kitchen. Immediately, I noticed a discomfort come over Bishnu's face. What just happened? Crap, did I just place Bishnu in an unfamiliar situation?

"Bishnu, please come with me. Sit down. I would like to buy you lunch as a thank you. Is that okay?"

"Oh, yes," he replied quickly as the discomfort melted away.

I understood at this moment that lunch was probably not an expense he could afford.

Earlier that day, I'd added up my own expenses for the twenty-one-day adventure:

Trekking Cost – $187

Trekking Permit - $33

Food & Lodging - $138

Replacement Camera - $23

The entire experience added up to a mere $358.00, of which the Fair Mount Trekking Shop received a whopping $187. That price included Bishnu as my personal guide for three weeks, a down sleeping bag, and a rented red jacket. I'm not sure how much of that money Bishnu actually received, so I would ensure he was well compensated and properly thanked.

For the next two hours, we played rummy and enjoyed our hot meals, mostly in silence. It was as if we were back on the trek together. Nothing was different between us, even though the landscape had shifted.

Halfway through the game, a wave of gratitude hit me as I watched Bishnu intensely review his cards before making his next move. What a changed man! All I could think of in that moment was how grateful I was that this stranger-for-hire had turned into a friend for life. Of all the guides I could have selected, it was Bishnu who won me over. Little did I know then that the name Bishnu is a Sanskrit name for boys meaning protector, and an important Hindu god. It all made perfect sense!

As a thank you, I had planned two gifts for Bishnu. The first was playing cards for fun, not necessarily to win. The pride and joy written across Bishnu's face when he reached 500 points first was precious. But there was one more priceless moment to come.

With lunch over and a new rummy champion declared, the moment of a final goodbye arrived. My heart was in my throat as I spoke. "Bishnu, thank you," was all I could muster before getting choked up. I was shaking. I pointed to his heart, and somehow the words began to flow.

"You helped me not to quit when things got hard. Thank you!"
"You taught me to trust that everything works out. Thank you!"
"You showed me how the moment matters most. Thank you!"
"You encouraged me to try new things. Thank you!"
"You kept me safe. Thank you!"

"Please accept this gift from my heart to yours." I slid into his hands a white three-by-five envelope which held two crisp twenty-dollar bills – twenty percent of the trekking cost. By the ecstatic look on Bishnu's face, along with the widest full teeth smile I'd ever seen, I knew Bishnu understood I was grateful for all that he had done.

While it may not have been customary to hug the tour guide at the end of a trip, I didn't care what rules I was breaking. In my country and my Italian family traditions, we hugged – and hugged a lot!

And just like that, Bishnu disappeared from my life. No forwarding mailing address, no email address, and certainly no cell phone number for either of us back in 1999.

Two days later, I received a package at the hotel's front desk. Given that I didn't know where I was sleeping from night to night, I was extremely curious to know who the mystery gifter was and how they knew where to find me.

Inside the woven sack were two items, but no note. I pulled out a beautiful brass, hand-held Bharat Haat prayer wheel, approximately seven inches long with a two-inch diameter spinning wheel. Carved within the wheel were unrecognizable symbols (mantras, I believe) along with small turquoise and coral stones. During our trekking days, Bishnu and I would spin the larger prayer wheels positioned outside villages or sacred sites. It is believed that when you spin prayer wheels, it is the same as saying prayers aloud. Lord knows I spun every visible prayer wheel I came across on the Annapurna Circuit.

I was a bit shocked to find the second item – a knife. The front desk person caught my startled reaction and quickly explained its great mythical importance within the Nepalese culture. The khukuri (Kukri) is symbolic of the Nepal Army and of all Gurkha regiments throughout the world. He told me it also signifies courage and valor of the bearer.

After hearing this explanation, I was brought to tears. Each of these gifts was extremely symbolic, deeply meaningful, and very costly. These had to be from Bishnu.

The next day, I returned to the Fair Mount Trekking Shop, where I'd found Bishnu three weeks earlier. The same old man who had greeted me back then remembered me. I told him how amazing the trek was thanks to Bishnu, and that I had returned to the store to thank Bishnu again. This man didn't need to know about the gift situation.

Unfortunately, the owner informed me that Bishnu left the day before for another trek. He would not return to Pokhara for at least two weeks.

I wanted to thank Bishnu one more time for helping me change. On the trail, I discarded parts of myself that were no longer needed in my life. At the same time, I found parts of myself that I promised I would always treasure, nurture, and continue to develop.

That same night, March 23, I emailed my family and friends to tell them I was heading back to Bangkok: I'm psyched that I've completed the trek, proud that I didn't give up, and beyond curious to see what unexpected experience awaits me next. Without a doubt, this experience was truly the hardest thing I ever accomplished on so many levels.

Up to that point in my life…

REFLECTION ON E: THE ANSWER

CERTAINTY ANNIHILATES CURIOSITY
That's a guarantee you can be certain of
So, will you stay limited by certainty or
Expand into the unknown with curiosity

When we are open to new possibilities
We are receptive to a new source
That new source fuels new ideas and ignites our hearts
New ideas and an open heart generate alternative choices
Alternative choices manifest new experiences
New experiences expand the edges of our growth zone

When we are closed to new possibilities
We are opposed to a new source
Choosing to cling only to what we want to know
Our source becomes stagnant, stale, and soon scarce
The scarcity generates irrational thoughts and fears
The irrational thoughts and fears limit actions and experiences
Limited actions and experience stop growth
Without growth, we die.

After reading the travels and trials associated with E – Experience Without Expectations – do you still believe that having certainty and guarantees are the best choices for you? I'll leave you with these three questions to ponder. Hopefully, they will entice you to consider choosing curiosity over certainty more often. You only have an extraordinary life to gain or miss out on.

- What would you do right now, without hesitation, if you did not need to have the perfect answer to act?
- What experiences would you have more often if you made choices free of certainty and guarantees?
- What would you do more of if you tapped into your Traveler's Heart regularly vs. only on an annual vacation, a long weekend, or a much-needed day off?

Chiang Rai and Monks from the Golden Triangle

Julie A. Zolfo

Adventures in Laos & the Mekong River

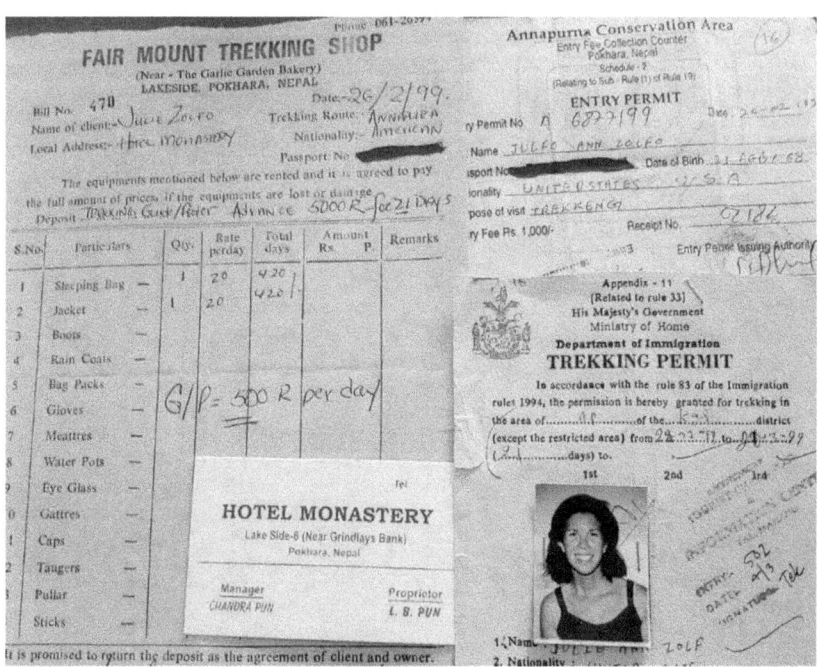

Annapurna trek permits, supplies and guide costs

Julie A. Zolfo

Guide Bishnu, majestic views, sleeping quarters

March 12, 1999, Thorong La Pass, Nepal
Trekked to 5,416 m (17,769 ft)
Celebrated a "Rummy 5,025" win & Grandpa's 90th birthday

Bishnu Memories: Cards, Map, Knife, Prayer Wheel

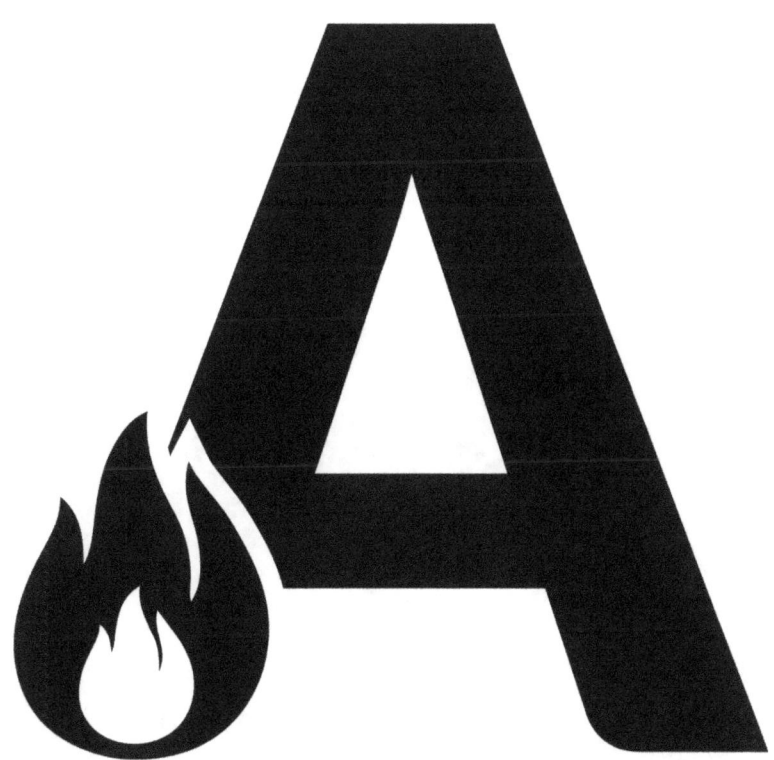

WISDOM:
ADVERSITY ACCELERATES SELF-EVOLUTION

DESIRE:
COURAGE

ADVERSITY MEANS AN instance of difficulty or misfortune. Overcoming adversity means to be successful despite challenges. Often, the obstacles that obstruct our progress are ones we place carefully in our path, thinking they are the safest or only choices available, or the ones that are acceptable and expected by family or society. And then there are the challenges that are beyond our control, which often involve our or a loved one's health, the economy, the environment, or natural disasters.

When we pass through adversity and land on the other side – either on our feet or merely picking ourselves up and dusting ourselves off for another try – we look back and consider what we could have done differently. The answer might be nothing. The experience might have shaped you into the stronger and more capable person you are today. You may have loved the experience while you were living it. Or it may have been unavoidable because it involved outside forces.

Like stress, people see adversity as negative. However, adversity does not mean failure, and it doesn't always mean hitting rock bottom. Challenges don't have to stop you from progressing at an even, steady pace. The answer might be asking for assistance in the beginning stages of a challenge before it becomes more problematic. Other people have been through what you are going through and listening to their stories and experiences might be all you need to get past your adversity. There are answers to your questions that you might not be aware of until you seek them.

I, myself, might have navigated my obstacles differently if I had known how to apply and practice the coaching tools, disciplines, and philosophies that I have since studied and mastered through several certifications.

And so, the adventure ends... In retrospect, I should have kept a journal when I returned to America and what I thought was "real life." In January 1999, I took a sabbatical from my job, left all of my belongings and my apartment with my roommate, and set off with a very oversized backpack and a passport to the other side of the world. My first stop was Thailand, and in August of that same year, my last stop was Ireland. There were plenty of adventures in between, and I logged almost every joyous minute of it in journals and emails. I even recorded the moments that weren't joyous, like freezing on the mountain in waist-deep snow (I hate the cold) and worrying if I was going to survive.

Somehow in all of that adventure and excitement, I forgot the word "sabbatical." I forgot I could go back to San Francisco. So, looking back to the fall of 1999, I didn't have to move to New York City. Yet, somehow, I thought I needed to.

New York City represented success to me. I took to heart the phrase "If you can make it there, you can make it anywhere." While still on my nine-month sabbatical, I met family and friends when they joined me in different European countries. I felt judged. I felt like they were wondering what I was going to do next when I got back to the real world. No one actually asked that, but I felt it. I let that feeling get into my head.

So, when I got off the plane in August 1999, I went home to New Jersey and started looking for a job. Everyone was urgently getting ready for Y2K. Jobs were plentiful in the dotcom industry, and I got one. It was a job in the travel and tourism department of the biggest internet sales company in New York City – two things I believed I wanted and needed (though it turns out they weren't).

I can still feel the heaviness and despair that enveloped me during that time. One cold winter night, I walked through the Port Authority. The shops were closed, and the other commuters had gone home long ago. My new job didn't seem to have a quitting time. As I passed one of the dark shops, I caught sight of my drawn reflection in the window. How did I get here? Why did I get here? Wasn't I already here?

In response to those questions, I got an apartment in New York City. I thought it was the commute that was bringing me down. But moving into my own apartment in the city was only a bandage to cover up the sore that was getting bigger. My coworkers were former Wall Street brokers who were used to the fast-paced, money-reaching, make-it-or-break-it life of the next win. That wasn't me. It also wasn't the mindset of the travelers I spent months within Southeast Asia. This, too, brought me down. I thought the only way to fix it was to get a different job.

My new job in the university recruiting industry was perfect for me. It involved travel – something I loved and was good at. From the outside, I was living the life that was idealized in movies and television shows: a thirtysomething, single female making lots of money and living in her own apartment in the Upper East Side. And it only took me eighteen months to get there. It was February 2001, and I finally seemed settled and content.

But that contented bubble was about to burst. A friend from college mentioned that she still talked to my ex-boyfriend. When Stacey mentioned Glenn's name, I caught my breath. Our relationship had a sour ending, and it took me a while to move on. My friend mentioned him very casually and asked me if she could give him my contact information. I hesitated a moment before laughing and telling her yes. Why not?

I didn't see any issue because I was different now. I remembered how much fun we'd had at the beginning of our relationship. And he lived in Arizona while I lived in New York City. I was curious. What could be the harm in a saying hello?

At the end of February, he emailed me. Seeing his name in my inbox made my heart skip. I didn't hesitate to answer him. Almost immediately, our former banter returned. It felt familiar, comfortable, and fun. For the first time in eighteen months, it felt like Zolfo Woman was back.

I felt strong. The girl who had her heart broken in her twenties was a bad memory. This thirtysomething gal was approaching this relationship differently. Also, Zolfo Woman was now living in her own apartment in The City That Never Sleeps and succeeding at a job with a lot of responsibilities. I felt a surge of pride as I recanted stories to Glenn about my solo trip halfway around the world with only a backpack and a passport.

Things moved fast after that first email. The first flowers from Glenn arrived in March, after I had a terrible biking accident that resulted in a concussion and a broken collarbone. Because of our past, we had not told anyone that we were speaking again. When my mom came into the city to check on me, she saw the flowers.

"Glenn? Glenn… Glenn?" she kept repeating.

"Yes." I offered no more.

After another month of emails and phone calls, we decided to see each other again. It had been eight years. Glenn was coming east for a trip home to Long Island. Not wanting to make a big-time commitment, we planned to meet for lunch. He called me from the cab telling me he was on his way. I felt butterflies, which were completely understandable when you are seeing an ex for the first time in almost a decade. He knocked on the door. I knew as soon as I opened it that life was never going to be the same.

From that afternoon in April 2001, the relationship took off. During that time, I was traveling extensively with my job, and I used frequent-flyer miles to cheaply and frequently visit Glenn. We met in Scottsdale, Sedona, and Lake Tahoe. We were having fun. The relationship progressed as much as it could with us living thousands of miles apart.

The distance wore on Glenn after a few months. "I can't do this anymore." I thought he meant the relationship, but he meant the commute. I was so afraid of losing him again that I offered to leave my job, my apartment, and my family and relocate to Arizona. I moved in with Glenn in August, less than six months after our reunion in New York.

My family and friends, who remembered picking up the pieces of me after the first breakup, thought I was moving too fast. They suggested we slow it down a little. I ignored their concerns, thinking I knew better than everyone else. I thought I was blissfully living that other Hollywood story – the second chance at an old romance.

For the first time, I thought that marriage and a family were a real possibility. I wanted to move this relationship along, and the only way I could see doing that was by moving to Arizona. I was an independent woman, and I was making a choice I felt was best for me and my relationship.

I thought of life as a checklist. I had traveled the world. Check! Lived in New York City. Check! Worked at a Fortune 100 company. Check! And next on the list was a relationship. Check?

I remember the day I moved in. His former roommate came by to drop off the key. As he left, I joked. "Your bachelor days just walked out the door."

But it was my independence that had just walked out the door.

In a clichéd life, hindsight is 20/20. The move to Arizona seemed like the natural thing to do because moving was one of my "things." In eight years, I had crisscrossed the country. After college, I lived in New Jersey while commuting into the city. When I was twenty-five, two of my friends moved to San Francisco. I followed them, thinking, "Why not?" My frequent travels also felt like moving. I felt like I was being bold and taking risks by never staying in one place too long.

But what I thought was a continuation of my adventures was actually a disruption. In Arizona, I met a series of barriers that felt like failures. I quickly found a job, but when the contract ended, I wasn't able to find another full-time job that best fit my ambitions and desires. I lost confidence, which resulted in slowly losing myself. The person who carried the backpack through the mountains of Nepal seemed further and further away each day. And it didn't help that it seemed like Glenn had the Midas

Touch. Everything he touched, career-wise, turned to gold. Everything I literally touched broke: his car, his washing machine, his oven.

My only acquaintances were Glenn's friends. I didn't have my own friends except for one, Seana. My childhood friend Kathleen had connected us to each other. But having one semi-new friend was difficult when I was losing myself.

Then there was the scorpion bite. One night as I was getting into the hot tub, a scorpion stung my toe. Being stung is not uncommon, though my reaction was. It went far beyond the moderate stinging, burning, and numbing sensations. My tongue felt five feet thick, my vision became blurry to the point of feeling blind. I spent the night in the ER, curled in a fetal position and believing I was going to die.

With all this adversity, my relationship suffered as well. After two years, Glenn and I were not getting along. The person he fell in love with was slowly fading, and neither of us liked the person I was becoming. There wasn't room in the relationship for this new person.

Mustering my sense of adventure and hoping to find some piece of the Julie who existed before Arizona, I planned a two-week motorcycle trip with Glenn. We explored the Sierra Nevada mountains of northern California, then continued down the Pacific Coast Highway before darting east across the Mojave Desert, then back home to Tempe. But the trip only made us realize we were ending, and that I was becoming less functional. Less functional and highly emotional. It didn't take much longer for me to spiral downward, fast, and hard. I was so disconnected from participating in life at every level. I wasn't working. I wasn't eating. I wasn't talking. But I was drinking, which only added gas to the fire.

At my lowest point, I found myself curled up in that familiar fetal position in the back bedroom, crying uncontrollably and rocking myself back and forth. Glenn sat on the floor next to me, doing the best he could to console me. But nothing he did comforted me.

No one could have comforted me.

I moved out shortly after that trip, but I did not leave Arizona until seven months later. During that time, I was still hoping that Glenn would ride up on his motorcycle and rescue me.

How did I get here? What happened to Zolfo Woman who trekked the Himalayas? Why did I now need rescuing?

It was then that I realized I had to leave Arizona if I was going to survive.

This was not the Hollywood ending I was expecting.

My friend Kathleen got on a plane and helped pick up the pieces of me the best she could. We packed my belongings into my Isuzu and headed north. We sat on a mountain peak in Sedona, eating sandwiches and planning our trip back east. I was going to my older sister Deana's house in Cary, North Carolina.

The memories of that time are not all my own. I was in a dark place with no air and no lights. I was stuck inside my brain and body, which were both slowly shutting down. Kathleen later filled in the gaps about my emotional state during the road trip. Her recall and perspective of my behavior is important to share because it shines a bright light on how fragile and unstable I became for that short period of time. Kathleen's narrative is included here:

I loved Sedona because we actually got to sightsee. It was my first time in Arizona, and sitting on that ridge, eating a great vegetarian sandwich made me so happy. We also walked to the Chapel of the Holy Cross and said a prayer. Then we got on the road. We needed to drive north to pick up Route 66.

We were at a crossroads ready to start out, and you sardonically asked, "Do you have to go stand on a corner in Winslow?"

I had no idea what you were asking.

"A lot of people when they visit have to do the lyrics of the song."

I said no, but silently sang the song in my head. It had never occurred to me. All that was important was getting you home. Well, to your new home.

Because I was not stable enough to drive in the dark, we only drove during the day. It took us four days to cross the United States.

It was really weird. That is the only way I can describe it. Weird. You were very militant about keeping track of our daily mileage and how much we spent. I knew you kept track of your spending on your nine-month trip, but there was something different about this.

One day I was standing at the pump, and you yelled to me from the driver's side through the passenger's window, "How much? How much was the gas?"

"What are you doing?"

"I am keeping track of what we spend."

When I told you the price, you pulled out a small notebook and feverishly wrote down what the price was.

"What are you doing?"

"I told you that I am keeping track of what we spend."

"What are you really doing?"

"Glenn told me that I am wasting my money flying you out and driving across the country and then flying you back home to New Jersey. He said that it would have been cheaper and faster to have my car shipped and fly by myself to North Carolina."

"Well, stop."

And you did.

We followed old Route 66 without stopping to sightsee. I had a mission, and that was to get some place where I felt safe.

It was like divine intervention in Albuquerque, New Mexico. I had never been there, either. My grandma lived there when her mother was dying of TB. She rode a mule to school and the mule would come back at the end of the day to pick up her and her brother. A stranger was passing through town and set up camp just down from my grandma's house. A neighbor told the stranger it was okay to camp there, but please be respectful because the children in the house just lost their mother.

The stranger was a sculptor. Before he left, he made an angel out of clay, and it was used as my great grandmother's grave marker. I just wanted to stay in the town a little longer because of the connection. Something I ate at dinner bothered me, so you allowed us to have a lazy morning and walk around town. Definitely someone intervened, because my stomach was miraculously better after you suggested we stay on through a late breakfast.

When we were driving through Oklahoma you asked, "Do you want to visit the bomb site?"

Just like the question about Winslow, Arizona, I had no idea what you were talking about. I just said no. When I figured it out later, I still was glad I said no. I didn't need to see it.

In Nashville, the home of many good restaurants, we ate at a Waffle House. Now mind you, I had never been to this famous chain restaurant. However, I had never been to Nashville, either. I guess I still haven't.

I drove each morning when I felt fresh. Kathleen took the wheel in the afternoons. As we drove east, the winter days got dark earlier, and we tried to not stay on the road too much after dark. In February 2004, cell phones with internet connections were just thoughts in an engineer's dreams a few thousand days away. So, each afternoon, we estimated the time we wanted to stop for the night, then picked up a magazine to find a AAA-recommended hotel. It was a little like hiking through Nepal. But that is where the similarity ended. When I left Nepal, I still had hope.

On February 10, 2004, one day before my thirty-sixth birthday, I arrived at my sister's house where she lived with her wife and seven-month-old daughter. I stayed in the basement guest room and cried and slept.

I often refer to the time after the road trip with Kathleen as "living in my sister's basement." With words and expressions, I paint an awful picture of a dark, unfinished space with a cot in the corner near the washer and dryer, past the old skis and tennis rackets. But it actually was a beautiful, finished downstairs living area with a bedroom, a family room, a home office, and a bathroom. It was a place where I found safety to heal. A space that provided space. I should have looked at it as the guest bedroom that offered privacy from the rest of the house and its occupants. However, the words I used fit my state of mind.

My niece, Alyssa, was actively crawling and sometimes made her way to my bedroom door and tapped it open. Her smile was contagious and allowed me to move out of my wallowing to play with her. Babies don't ask anything of you. They only want their needs met. I could take her for walks. I could play on the floor. I could even nap when she napped. My sister-in-law worked from home, so I was not responsible for the care of my niece, but I think my niece was the person responsible for the care of my heart.

One afternoon in early May, I awoke from a nap to a quiet house. My sister and her wife were upstairs, and the baby was still napping. As usual, my nap had been preceded by crying, which led to a numbness and an exhaustion-induced sleep. Waking slowly, I lay in my bed with a sleep-foggy brain and heard a question.

"Where were you last happy?"

Unstartled, I paused for a second and answered out loud. "San Francisco."

The voice very distinctly said, "Then go back to San Francisco."

I heard my sister moving around in the kitchen, and I took the stairs two at a time in my race to get to her. She greeted me with her usual warm smile, one I can still count on today.

"Hi. What's up?"

"I need to go to San Francisco."

In a calm, curious voice, she said, "May I ask why you need to go to San Francisco?"

"It was the last place I was happy."

I felt a spark of hope as we made plans. I called my friends in San Francisco and booked a flight. Part of the plan was to visit them and see if I could go back.

From there, it felt like a snowball picking up momentum as it rolled. The beautiful snow that made the snowball bigger was my spirit coming back to life. I got to San Francisco and felt my body sigh. It felt like home.

Three weeks later, I stood outside my friend Christine's apartment. My belongings arrived before I did. I looked at the three moving boxes in her foyer and said, "My life has been narrowed down to three boxes". We laughed.

How did I get here? I heard the voice. I listened to the voice. I came for a visit. It felt like the place I needed to be. And I moved once again.

I overcame my adverse circumstances, which were the lowest and loneliest days of my life. And I learned how to push through the darkness to find myself again. The strong, independent, fearless, smart, and practical traveler who woke up each morning with a light heart ready to take on the next mountain was back.

REFLECTION ON A: ARE YOU READY TO TAKE ON YOUR MOUNTAIN?

BY NOW, YOU can see why millions of people like myself use travel for personal growth, healing, and transformation. Travel allows you to encounter the unfamiliar, the unplanned, the unseen, and the unknown – those unexpected experiences which travelers gladly pay for, brag about, search out, and encourage others to find. Living outside your comfort zone is inescapable when you travel.

So, here's The Traveler's H.E.A.R.T. paradox… Why do you fall apart when these same "uns" appear in your daily life after you return home? Contrary to conventional thinking, you don't need to quit your job and backpack for years to find courage for your advantage and advancement in life.

> "Victory over others brings us satisfaction, but victory over ourselves brings us joy."
> ~ Dr. David R. Hawkins, *POWER vs FORCE: The Hidden Determinants in Human Behavior*

To overcome life's challenges and breakdowns, you must release your reliance on old patterns; otherwise, it's impossible to calculate a new reality. I know this because I did it. Only by applying the same level of Zolfo Woman courage to my biggest life challenges did I learn how to let adversity change me instead of me trying to change the adversity.

So, are *you* ready to break free from your limiting thinking so you can experience more of what you want from life? Using this list of empowering Break Free mantras, choose a new, courageous, and bold alternative action.

- Right now, break free from blame and own your actions.
- Right now, break free from being right and just do the right thing.
- Right now, break free from the approval of others, and honor and respect yourself.
- Right now, break free from anger and forgive with a peaceful mind.
- Right now, break free from fear and trust your gut instincts and intuition.
- Right now, break free from mistakes and learn from every opportunity.
- Right now, break free from being perfect and take action. Make progress.
- Right now, break free from self-doubt and confidently follow your passions.
- Right now, break free from being too sensitive and be powerfully vulnerable.
- Right now, break free from what is comfortable and be deliberately daring.

Which statement resonates most with you?

Is there more than one?

My recommendation: pick the one that *yells* to you and start there.

THE motorcycle

Finding my smile again with the help of my niece

2,160-mile road trip to NC with BFF Kathleen

Happy times with my SF Green's Sport Bar Family

Christine's note of hope when I returned to SF, CA

WISDOM:
RECALCULATE WHAT MATTERS MOST

DESIRE:
CLARITY

RECALCULATE WHAT MATTERS most.

A modest thought, but bold enough to become a mantra.

Recalculate what matters most.

The art of recalculating is taking new data and calculating again.

Recalculate what matters most.

- What to remove.
- What to retain.
- What to renew.

Recalculate what matters most.

Gain clarity. When you are clear about what you want, you are unconcerned with others' reactions.

Recalculate what matters most.

When did I first consciously apply this wisdom in my life?

2004 was a year of many changes, endings, and new beginnings. In February, I packed up and left what I felt was a failure in Arizona and retreated to my sister's basement in North Carolina. In June, I listened to my voice once again, and with strength and courage moved back to San Francisco. Feeling like I had the world at my feet and standing on more stable ground, I found a job doing what I do best – campus recruiter.

As a campus recruiter, I combined work with my love of travel. Even though the travel was domestic, I was constantly in different locations, learning new terrains and meeting new people. And because it was something I loved, I worked hard and got everything done. I felt as if I was at the top of my game.

As a seasoned recruiter, I felt more was expected of me. I pushed myself to work even harder, staying up late at night to finish reports and send emails to the organization's leadership, often after working fourteen-hour days. Many emails contained typos and mistakes, which is consistent with dyslexia, a condition I was diagnosed with immediately after graduating college in 1990. (How I ever graduated is another story.) I knew from past experience that when the dyslexic brain is tired or overwhelmed, there is a greater chance of errors. Worse yet, I'm unable to see minor mistakes that spell check misses.

In August 2007, on one of my rare non-travel days, my supervisor scheduled my half-yearly review. I referred to employee reviews as Tissue Box Days since my boss at PIER 39 jokingly said that, because people often cried during reviews, she kept a box of tissues handy.

When I headed into my review, I chuckled to myself about the Tissue Box Day because this firm also tended to make employees cry. We recruited and hired the best of the best. However, when you have a room full of the best of the best, everyone becomes average. When reviewed, these overachievers are measured on a scale they are not used to.

I tended not to cry because my reviews were typically good. Confident in my performance and work ethic, I expected to be completely satisfied with this review as well.

As I sat across from my supervisor, she looked through the papers and used the word "careless." The word stopped me. She was referring to my frequent mistakes and typos in emails and reports – especially those sent to management late at night.

I felt lightheaded. Careless. My trigger word. Careless. Throughout my primary and high school years, teachers often used the word careless to describe my work. Before I knew better, I had always perceived the label of "careless" as not smart enough. Even now, the word careless bothers and hurts me because I felt that I cared tons!

As my supervisor continued, I came back to the present and thought about the feedback I was receiving. She explained that I had six months until my next review. During that time, she expected me to work on my performance.

I walked out of her office stunned, but mostly ashamed. I was used to receiving gold stars.

Careless was not a word I would let be used for my work – or me – again. I pulled up my boots and put my head down to buck against the storm. I was determined to not have another mistake in my emails or reports, so I gathered an army of good friends throughout various time zones to check my work before I submitted it.

I also found the Davis Dyslexia Association. I learned that with my dyslexia, I should have either asked for an assistant to review long emails and reports or set better working hours to avoid being tired or overwhelmed so I'd have better concentration.

My next review was in February 2008. I was no longer ashamed. There was a pep in my step, and I was a little cocky as I walked into my supervisor's office. I dared her to use the word careless. She immediately congratulated me for doing everything they'd asked of me.

That phrase made me sit up taller. I thought, "Everything they'd asked of me?" They may have meant this as praise, but the synapses in my brain started to speak to each other and I got mad.

Everything they'd asked of me?

Repeating it to myself made me madder. I had spent six months of my life sacrificing many hours to make sure everything was correct, double, and triple checking again, just to hear that I was good enough.

Holy crap!

It started to sink in. I was working to hear someone tell me I was good enough. How did I not know that for myself? How much of my life had I spent seeking outside validation?

This moment was the dawn of the Traveler's H.E.A.R.T. concept and the beginning of the wisdom "Recalculate what matters most." At this moment, I opened up to awareness and clarity.

"I am sorry, but could you stop there?"

She looked surprised.

I, too, was surprised. But the fog lifted. I quickly assessed my working life. I knew what I liked and didn't like in all my jobs. Also, I was single and wasn't responsible for anyone's happiness or well-being but my own.

I was shocked my sudden declaration, but I knew it was the right thing to do. I took a moment to weigh the consequences before I spoke. "I am no longer interested in doing this job, and I would like to give my six-month notice."

My supervisor went from shocked to understanding in less than five seconds. She said I had actually stayed longer in the job than most people did. With the extensive travel, people tended to burn out. But I liked the travel. It fueled me. I didn't like the rest of the job. I have since learned that if you loathe 80% of your job, it is not the right one for you, even if you are good at it.

The firm prided themselves on retention, so my supervisor encouraged me to look for another position within the company. It was the middle of the recruiting season, one that I had worked hard to prepare for and successfully manage. Because of my work ethic, I stayed in my current position for myself and to help train someone to transition into my role. However, two weeks later, there was a town hall led by our Human Resources Director, who spoke about the Internal Mobility Team.

My friend Denise sat in front of me at the presentation. She worked in that department. As soon as she told me about her job, I knew I wanted that job, too! And I knew it was supposed to be mine. I had never been so clear about anything.

More clarity in my life. This was my dream job. I got the title of being a coach.

I grew up watching Tony Robbins. My parents taught me about Warner Erhard and Og Mandino. When I was eleven years old, I read Og Mandino's book *The Choice* while on a family trip to California. I finished it on the plane ride, and I was hooked. One day, flipping through the newspaper as eleven-year-olds did in 1979, I saw that he would be lecturing at a hotel near my house. I asked my dad if we could attend.

That Saturday, sitting between my father and my cousin Robert, I knew. I knew that this was what I wanted to do. I wanted to motivate people. To me, Og was the greatest motivational speaker. I was eleven and hadn't seen any others, but I still stand by that opinion today.

The little girl sitting in that Fairfield Inn on Route 46 in New Jersey was bursting inside of me as I realized that, if I was going to be in Human Resources, this was the Human Resources job I wanted. I was going to be a motivator of people, coaching them to find their dream job. It was a huge step in the direction of my career desires.

To be the best at the job, I needed to learn more. So, I invested in a nine-month program to be a certified life coach at iPEC. Then the 2008 economic recession hit, and I was laid off. But I wasn't devastated. With a severance package to last me through the next nine months, I felt as if I was still on top of the world.

In the iPEC program, I learned about their Core Energy Coaching™ – a process that uncovers inner blind spots and cultivates new perspectives on a sustainable level. I loved learning how to coach people to dig deeply, honestly, and objectively into their energy and mental programming in order to assess who they are and who they want to become.

What made iPEC stand out among the other coaching programs was their trademarked attitudinal assessment, The Energy Leadership Index Assessment. The ELI gauges how a person approaches and reacts to different circumstances and experiences by producing a combined numerical value of spiritual, mental, emotional, and physical energy. This single factor, known as the Average Resonating Level of Energy, is a strong indicator of success in various aspects of work and life. It represents the average of all your energy levels, under both normal and stressful conditions. This was going to be the game-changer tool I could use to help my clients uncover insights on how they might experience each level of energy in the areas of:

- Finances,
- Leadership ability,
- Working relationships,
- Family relationships,
- Work/life balance,
- Health and wellness,
- Spiritual connection,
- Communication skills, and
- Productivity.

With a certificate in hand, I hit the pavement ready to find my next dream job, but the recession made it difficult. During my search, I found Cross-Cultural Solutions. Their program offered a volunteer experience to travel and make a difference with community engagement. There were opportunities to teach, offer healthcare, or perform social services.

I thought about what I enjoyed most about my travels, especially to Nepal, and what I considered my dream job. The voices in my head and heart always tried to remind me when I was my happiest. They whispered and sometimes even shouted, "You need to travel!"

So, I chose to go to New Delhi, India and teach conversational English to students and adults at the Okhla School, which was managed by the non-profit Vidya. I would leave in January 2010 and stay through April, teaching for one month and exploring for three.

After a year of many, sudden changes in my professional life, I felt confident in the changes I was making. My reasons for doing this were clear. First, I wanted to experience international volunteering. Second, I have a keen interest in fully immersing myself in a new culture, challenging my comforts and norms, in order to fully embrace new ways of living, behaving, and being. Third, I have a tireless passion to explore old worlds (cultures and religions) while seeking the beauty of the land through its sunsets and sunrises. I also wanted to understand where India's future was heading, both domestically and within the global markets. I planned to research and interview with companies that have major outsourcing investments in India.

I felt excited while planning this trip. I remembered this excitement from before. It was the freedom of movement. I could feel it in my heart. I was making the right decision.

With the support of my family and friends, I left San Francisco on January 27, 2010, and headed to New York to fly out of JFK. This would allow me time to connect with my best friend Terri, my former roommate and road trip buddy. I knew I needed a night with her before heading out to a trip that would change my life.

I flew out on Friday, January 29. When my feet hit the pavement outside the airport in New Delhi on January 30, I heard, "I am back!" There was that voice again. Mine. In that moment, wearing my bright blue T-shirt with VOLUNTEER stamped in big gold letters across the chest and looking around at the colors of India and its people, I heard what I needed to hear. "I've arrived!"

The ground felt strong beneath my feet. Standing in that spot outside the airport, I felt as if my life did a 180. The clarity of my choices filled my mind. I had felt this before. This freedom. Not a freedom *from* but a freedom *to*. A freedom to make the choices I wanted to make. I was going from the unconscious to the conscious, and it felt right.

I experienced an immediate sense of déjà-vu. Eleven years before, almost exactly to the day, I had landed in Bangkok, Thailand. The thirty-one-year-old woman who got off the plane on January 26, 1999 and traveled the world with her backpack was back. She might be a little older and roughed up around the edges, but Zolfo Woman was back.

JULIE CONQUERS INDIA....

The minivan that was waiting for me at the airport deposited me at my gated apartment complex. A man sitting in a booth got out when we neared; he lifted the wooden barrier to let us through. I already felt safe and pampered.

My home for the four weeks while I was teaching was a flat which Cross-Cultural Solutions provided to the volunteers. The flat (it sounds so sophisticated...) was a cross between a hostel and a dorm room. It had a living area, a kitchen, and three bedrooms which each had their own bathroom.

One of my major goals while in India was to truly live the native experience. I wanted to be immersed in the life and culture. One of my first observations was the color. Everything was bright – the clothes, the buildings... Even the food, which was savory, spicy, and very sweet. I felt as if I'd been living in a black-and-white television before then. But it wasn't just the scenery. My eyes were being opened to what I needed to know. The picture was clearer. I was finding clarity.

Seeing through clearer eyes began with the teaching experience, which I thought would come naturally for me. I was a recruiter; I was trained in public speaking. I was also a certified career coach. These skills made me a natural teacher – so I thought.

I'd be teaching English to teens and to an adult group of teachers. I was paired with another volunteer, Jody, and I was glad to not be embarking on the venture on my own. I thought the first day went well as I taught subjects and verbs. But it went downhill fast from there. For the next two days, the students met my lessons with nothing but blank stares. With my skills and experience, I didn't understand why I wasn't connecting with them. Thankfully, I discussed it with the other volunteers. They advised me that I needed to adjust my old ways. This was not the corporate world, and the students were not responding, so I had nothing to lose in trying a new method.

On the fourth day, I looked at the silent brown faces and became silly. Shedding each layer of the stiff, corporate presentation allowed me to be my true, authentic self.

The students' eyes opened wider and brighter with clarity – theirs and mine. All of us were learning. And we were having fun. Zolfo Woman was on center stage, and she was a hit!

I felt as if I had life under control. The first week of school was going much better, and when my flat mates suggested an excursion, I was eager to join them. We hired a driver for the weekend and set off to Agra to see the Taj Mahal. Our driver, Bobby, expertly navigated through the heavy traffic under the smog-thick skies. Crowds of buses, cars, bikes, mopeds, people, and cattle were not unusual, even on a Saturday morning. Bobby finally left the main roads and took us through "the scenic route," searching for a shortcut. During our five-hour drive, we traveled through very impoverished and remote areas before arriving in Fatehpur Sikri, a fortified ghost city once ruled by the Mughai Empire during Akbar's reign.

Stepping out of the car in Fatehpur Sikri, we were immediately engulfed by an aggressive sea of merchants and wanna-be tour guides. We were told that the area was a Muslim area, and it was best to have a guide. We trusted this advice and each contributed 100R ($2) for a guide, who taught us the history and importance of Fatehpur Sikri (which means City of Victory). The guide also kept the crowds of merchants at bay.

Bobby helped us find a safe place to eat and sleep for the night. We'd planned to visit the Taj Mahal the following morning, so we had the remainder of the afternoon and evening to explore our surroundings, which included the Sada Bazaar. Just imagine your typical weekend flea market. Now add a few dozen monkeys, several cows, and swarms of flies. Then include colorful people buying and selling Indian sweets, colorful clothes, and bike helmets.

It was a joyous, long day, and we were exhausted at the end. I was happy to get back to our hotel to clean up and snuggle down into the bed for a good night's sleep when BOOM! Fireworks exploded right outside our windows! They were so close; I thought I was going to be hit by ash. Then more fireworks. Then a marching band, followed by an hour-long duet in Hindi at a very high pitch.

It was a wedding! I had been hoping to be invited to a wedding while I was in India!

The next morning, my group met under the fluorescent-lit awning of the hotel. At 5:30 a.m., it was still dark. Most of us were still yawning, but we were quite excited to see one of the New Seven Wonders of the World, The Taj Mahal.

After a quick ride, Bobby left us at the box office. It was still dark, and only a few people were waiting. A gentleman approached us and instructed us on the items we were not allowed to bring into the Taj. The biggest no-no, or *nahai* in Hindi, was a pen or any other writing materials. The guards (with their guns) frowned on people writing "Julie was here" or "Ravi loves Bhati forever. XOXOX" on the marble walls.

Inside the box office were four windows: two for Indians (one male and one female), and two for tourists (one male and one female). My friend was first in line, right in front of me, in the female tourist line. When the clock struck opening time, the male Indians were admitted first. Then the female Indians. Then the male tourists. Then the female tourists. It did not matter that we had arrived first! I did want to be immersed in the Indian culture…

This slight was forgotten when we passed through the fortress wall and stopped in awe. The early morning sunlight shone on the most magnificent building ever built. And it was built for love. At the time, I did not know the love story behind the construction of the Taj Mahal in honor of wife number three.

We toured the grounds for two and a half hours. I remember the feeling of the white marble under my hand. It was a moment I will forever savor.

The time I spent teaching seemed to fly by. In four short weeks, these wonderful people opened their hearts, their school, and their lives, embracing me wholly. When I left, I felt complete. I had a new clarity. Alongside the poverty, the chaos, and the pollution of India, my passion for teaching was reinforced. I knew that when I got home, my path was to combine my corporate recruiter skills, my training experience, and my coaching certification to empower and inspire others.

When I left Delhi to travel within India, I wrote on my travel blog, "Let the adventure begin." Coincidence? I wrote that the last time I was becoming clear on what I wanted. In New Zealand, my taste for travel was awakened. In India, *I* was awakened. And this awakened state was my new reality. The adventure can end, but the lessons would be incorporated into my daily life. This is the Traveler's H.E.A.R.T.

From the beginning of this journey, my intention was to participate in something that was bigger than myself. I was in a rut. I was stale and board with the "norms" of life: get a good job, have a nice home, eat at the new restaurant, buy the latest fashion. It all left me feeling numb.

My dad, always the wise one, continuously challenged me whenever I was in the same rut. "Julie, what are you passionate about?" he asked. "When you find that passion, you will never be bored."

INDIA CONQUERS, BUT DOESN'T DEFEAT, JULIE

In three weeks, I visited four of India's twenty-eight states: Rajasthan, Uttar Pradesh, West Begal, and Chennai (Madras).

I flew from New Delhi to Jodhpur. As the plane landed, I peered out my window at the desert landscape. It looked as if I was flying into Sky Harbor Airport in Arizona. There was the mountain that looked like Camelback Mountain, the familiar desert, and the welcoming blast of heat. However, the face-to-face meeting with the military force as we landed confirmed that I was, indeed, not in Arizona.

I stayed in Jodhpur, the Blue City, for only a few days. The city has tiny streets; I could touch the buildings on both sides with my outstretched arms while riding in the back of the rickshaw. I visited Mehrangarh Fort, which is still run by the family today. The audio tour lasted three hours. I enjoyed the stunning terracotta, the latticed exterior, the adorned seats on top of the elephants, the Palki Khana (private enclosures that women arrived in town in), the views of the city, and the Marwar Mini Paintings. In my wish to experience India, I was very glad to have this attraction on my list.

After Jodhpur, I took a train to Jaisalmer, the Golden City. The trip, starting at my hotel in Jodhpur, was like a scene out of a movie. You know the ones in which everything bad happens to the heroine – she lands in ditches, her roof leaks, and spiders come out of the walls – but she looks beautiful throughout the whole film and eventually finds a knight on a big white steed who carries her off to her happy ending? Well... I had all the mishaps. I can't say I looked beautiful with wispy hair the whole time. And the person saving me at the end of the film? I would say wait and see, but there is only one person still standing at the end of this motion picture. That is me. But please come along for the ride.

At 5:30 p.m., I told the hotel staff that I needed to meet my train at 11 p.m. The Holi celebration was still filling the streets, so the staff suggested I leave as soon as possible. I thought that timeline might be a tad too precautionary, but I trusted the locals and went to my room to repack my bags, prepared to sit at the train station for many hours.

At 6:20 p.m., I headed back to the front desk. The hotel owner said that I would not find a rickshaw because of the celebration and that I should walk to the station. This time I did not trust the local, so I argued and urged him to find me a ride. He stood his ground. I had no other choice. (I should have listened to the voice beating up from below the chaos – the voice from the pages of my New Zealand journal. "Choice!" I should have remembered that I always have a choice.)

At 6:45 p.m., with my backpacked tightly secured, I took off. The Holi revelers jostled me as they rushed through the streets. I was a little unnerved, worried that I couldn't walk all the way to the train station with a pack on my back. Then my prayers were answered. I saw an available rickshaw driver just twenty yards ahead. Even better, he saw me! We made the connection. I had a ride. I moved forward. But I was stopped. A very agitated, very large cow – with horns – came between me and the rickshaw. I did not have a chance…

WHACK! The cow pinned me against the blue walls. In shock, I tried fending off the beast. It would not move. My driver looked at me with pity. He could not get through the throng of celebrants to help me. Then the crowd stepped in – the same crowd I was a little nervous about before. *Thank you, angels!* They brushed the animal away, and I ran to the rickshaw. "Train station now, please!"

In the movie version, I think I'd be played by Emma Stone.

At 7:00 p.m., I deposit myself safely at the station.

At 11:20 p.m., I sat in my sleeper car, beginning a six-hour train ride. I spent that time sleeping and praying. Two prayers: one of thanks and the other of hope and blessings.

At 5:05 a.m., I stood on the platform in Jaisalmer, looking for my ride. A man whom I met at the train station the night before asked me if I needed a ride. I told him that the guesthouse where I was staying, Shahi Palace, was sending someone to retrieve me. The woman standing behind me said that she was staying at the same location and waiting for the same driver.

The woman, Susan, and I exchanged greetings and gave quick introductions. Susan was also American, and also from San Francisco. She also lived in the Marina. Absolutely crazy! I'd traveled halfway around the world to meet my neighbor. She worked as a pharmacist at the Safeway I used. We'd definitely met before. *Thank you, angels.*

At 5:25 a.m., our driver had still not shown up. Susan and I were barraged with rickshaw drivers wanting us to ride with them. One told us that the owner of the establishment was out too late celebrating Holi and could not meet us. We didn't believe him.

The crowds began to thin. We had been waiting for thirty-five minutes, so we decided to ride with two Indian gentleman who said they were from the building next to our destination. We were tired and our defenses were down. Feeling like we had no choice (there is that word again), we hopped into their jeep with four other Westerners – all males.

At 5:45 a.m., the driver stopped at a guesthouse that was clearly not our destination. The Westerners got out and the driver invited us in for tea. He started to take my backpack with him. Susan and I refused to get out of the car and demanded that they drive us to Shahi Palace as promised.

After some Hindi exchange with his companion that we did not understand, the men took us down a dark road. We told the driver how angry we were. He stopped the jeep and yelled, "I don't need your money! Get out!"

Shit!

As this exchange took place, a rickshaw driver came along. Another angel sent to us. We got into his rickshaw with our bags, and he drove us to Shahi Palace.

At 5:55 a.m., we arrived at our destination. Frazzled. Upset. But safe!

The staff explained that their driver got to the station late. Two other women got into his jeep, and he figured we would find our way to the hotel. Which we did. But we were still mad.

They gave us their finest room to sleep in until breakfast, promising they would sort out everything.

Are you still seeing Emma Stone?

Fast forward twelve hours later.

At 6:00 p.m., Susan and I sat on the rooftop overlooking the city, drinking Kingfisher beer, and thinking about the day we'd spent sightseeing and enjoying each other's company.

Lessons learned:
- Listen to your gut.
- When the driver does not show up, pay for a private driver.
- Never get into a truck with two men when you don't speak their language. Even if you are traveling with another female.
- There is always a choice.

Before I left San Francisco, I researched unique adventures in the Lonely Planet Guidebook on India. A camel trek and safari in Jaisalmer had caught my attention. I couldn't think of a better way to celebrate surviving my trip to Shahi Palace, than with a two-day camel trek into the desert just thirty miles from the India/Pakistan border.

Three other guests at Shahi Palace signed up for the trek: Dennis from Minnesota, and Fumio and Umee from Osaka, Japan. We exchanged hellos and got into the jeep for the ride.

By 11:30 a.m., after a few stops for sightseeing, I was anxious to start the adventure.

And so, it began…

My camel's name was Papaya, and my ten-year-old guide was Gesko. He was the tiniest old soul – a man at the ripe age of ten!

We mounted our camels and enjoyed a one-hour ride through the desert, which still reminded me of the Arizona landscape. But I was on a camel. I was not in Arizona anymore.

After that first hour, we set up camp for lunch. This was a welcome relief to my bottom. The group chatted while our guides prepared our lunch of dal, rice, and bread. It was amazing to watch them cook over a tiny fire. Then we sat and watched them clean up. Then we sat and waited while the tired camels rested. Then we sat for another three and a half hours. This was not the adventure I'd signed up for.

Finally getting back on the camels, we rode for another hour and a half to our campsite among the sand dunes. That was the *Arabian Nights* scene I was waiting to experience! Camels and sand dunes!

We were given time to explore the dunes, which were magical. And I did not lose the worth of the moment. There was no one else around us. We were the only people among the vastness of the dunes, sky, and sand.

Even though there was the magic, I still expressed my slight disappointment in the lengthy afternoon break that left us with little riding time. Our guides replied, "You are our guest. We make you happy." They arranged a sunset ride through the dunes to compensate. It worked. It was magical.

After the sunset ride, our guides prepared dinner for us again. The sky was dark. We only had the campfire and the stars to light the evening. The guides sang songs around the campfire. It was like being in a movie. We retired at 10:15, just as the moon rose and lit up the night sky. I turned toward the west and saw a glowing city. I asked what the lights were and was told it was the India/Pakistan border. I didn't ask if the white flashes in the night sky were shooting stars or missiles. I chose to believe that they were magical stars.

The next day, Fumio and Umee headed back while Dennis and I set out on another trek with our two young guides (aged ten and sixteen). These two boys led us through the desert, stopping only for a lunch break. Dennis and I offered to help. We chopped vegetables with a dull knife, washed dishes with sand, and ate our yummy dal among a mass of flies that swarmed around us. It was glorious.

India is not for the weak or pampered traveler. There are many things one needs to overlook, or the experience will be polluted with judgments and "should bes." For me, the joys of traveling are to immerse myself and experience all of it. And during the camel trek/safari, I truly felt at one with India. I highly recommend this type of adventure for those who seek something unique and different.

In my journal I wrote, If I needed to leave India after this experience, I would leave with a mind and spirit filled with much gratitude and blessings… but thankfully there is even more to experience.

I truly believed that. But I didn't realize what it foreshadowed…

I left Jaisalmer by train and made my way to Jaipur. There was a slight miscommunication in my arrival date, and they had given away my room. I negotiated a rate and stayed in a room that was being renovated. I was becoming more confident and didn't let minor complications become problems. In Jaipur, I enjoyed sightseeing at the temples. At the guesthouse, I was invited to experience their prayer service. I was adorned with red dye and rice on my forehead and then permitted to make an offering and/or blessing. It was a beautiful experience to sit among the devoted, with permission to observe. This was one of the main reasons I chose India. What a wonderful gift.

My next destination was Udaipur. Just a train ride away. By this time, I was becoming an experienced India traveler, and my arrival in Udaipur was flawless. When I got off the train, a tall Indian man held a sign with my name on it.

When I got to the guesthouse, the manager said, "We have been waiting for your arrival and have saved you the best room."

This was going to be an extra fabulous experience.

Udaipur is known as the Venice of the East, or the City of Lakes because of the lakes and lush hills of the Aravallis. With its fascinating blend of sights and sounds, it is often an inspiration for poets, writers, and painters.

During my time in India, I relied heavily on other travelers for their advice regarding where to go and what to see next. The must-sees near Udaipur were Ranakpur and Kumbhalgarh.

Fort Kumbhalgarh is a Mewar fortress that was built in the 15th century by Rana Kumbha. It was enlarged through the 1800s and occupied through the 19th century. It is now open to the public as a museum. It was the most important fort in Mewar after The Chittaurgarh.

The fort has perimeter walls that extend thirty-six kilometers in length, claimed to be the longest in the world after the Great Wall of China. What I found most interesting were the 360 temples within the fort. 300 of the temples were Jain, and the rest were Hindu. I felt honored to walk among them.

The next day, I visited Ranakpur. On the way, I stopped for a roadside lunch of roti and chai. I was being very cautious with my stomach when it came to street food. In my journal, I wrote, *So far, so good.*

At Ranakpur, I had my first experience with a Jain temple. The temple is designed as a chaumukha, with four faces representing the four cardinal directions of the cosmos: North, South, East and West.

After two days of visiting the beautiful structures, and basking in their spirituality, I woke up early the next morning to take a yoga class – something I promised to do more of in India. I hoped to end my travels in Rishikesh, which is the biggest yoga center in India.

I left Ranakpur, feeling very uplifted, and headed to Varanasi. The city of Varanasi draws millions of people from around the world to dip in the holy Ganges for its power to absolve one from all sins. I did not have an overwhelming desire to visit Varanasi, but as my travels led me and I found more clarity, I discovered a path of spirituality that I followed throughout India. This path led me from city to city, temple to temple.

In Varanasi, I took a sunrise boat cruise that launched from the Ghats on the River Ganges. As I boarded the boat, a young girl offered me a lotus flower and a candle. Sitting on the boat at sunrise, with my lotus flower in hand, waiting to release it, was humbling and powerful at the same time.

In silence, I released my lotus flower and candle on the river, offering a prayer to those who have supported me.

The next day, still open to worship experiences, I traveled to Sarnath, where Buddha gave his first sermon. I felt blessed as I visited this holy land.

I returned to my guesthouse feeling very thankful for the experience and packed for my twenty-one-hour trip to Kolkata – which the owner of the guesthouse has suggested I visit. I had been avoiding train bathrooms up to that point, but I knew that I could not do so any longer. Just part of the trip.

As I settled onto the train for my long ride, a Sadhu – a holy man in India – placed something on my head without my permission. I know a blessing is a blessing, and I should have seen it that way, but I did not ask for it. Then when I tried to tip him ten rupees, he demanded fifty. Instead of fighting, because I had a long trip ahead of me and feared bad karma, I paid the man.

Surprisingly, I wasn't too exhausted when I reached Kolkata, and I set out to explore the city. I surveyed my surroundings with excitement. It was the first time in seven weeks that I saw no cow poop on the sidewalks. There were taxis, a skyline, a green urban park, and people dressed in western attire. It almost, very loosely, felt like New York City or London. Loosely.

I spent the day exploring the city and then made it an early night in my air-conditioned hotel room, awaiting my trip to Chennai the next day.

I'd planned this leg of the trip before I left home. I felt that fate was drawing me here. Just as I was confirming my plans to travel to India, I received a Facebook friend request from an old college friend, Marilyn. I hadn't heard from her in almost twenty years. She'd been living in India as an expat for six years. She stumbled on my name through a mutual friend and contacted me out of the blue. When I received the friend request, I yelled to my mother in another room, "Mom, it's a sign!"

I was anxious with excitement as I flew over the palm trees of Chennai. I had been anticipating a different vibe from southern India, and I felt immediately that I was right. When I stepped off the plane, feeling the warm tropic air on my face, Marilyn's driver greeted me. (Most expats in India have drivers because of the chaotic driving conditions.)

I was also anxious to see a friend I hadn't seen in over twenty years. I kept thinking...

Where did the time go?

What have I been doing?

Will I look twenty years older?

Marilyn opened her door and greeted me with a big hug. True friendship can last decades even when you don't see or speak to each other.

We sat on her couch, catching up before heading out to see the city and have dinner. We stopped at St. Thomas Church, which houses the tomb of the doubting disciple. We stood at the back and listened to the sermon. The priest spoke in the language native to the city but switched to English for a brief moment. I heard the words as clear as day: "God will provide."

My head shook. It was like in the movie *Field of Dreams* when Kevin Costner heard and saw messages that only a few others could. That is exactly how I felt. And the message I kept getting was the same.

I'd heard the message for the first time before I left for India. I was told, "You are going to be okay, and God will provide all that you need."

The day after hearing the priest, Marilyn and I saw the movie *Avatar*. It was very reflective for me. Similar to Jake Sully, I had fully immersed myself in an entirely different culture, which included different ways of being, thinking, and behaving. Also, the movie was very spiritual. The mother goddess, Eywa, has the wisdom of all the ancestors in the beyond. At one point in the movie it is said, "Eywa will provide." It gave me shivers. But I listened, and I believed.

Marilyn and I spent a few more days together. During our final meal, we had a loving and compassionate conversation about her spiritual journey that opened my eyes to wonderful and deeper thinking. It was a blessing and a true gift to be in Marilyn's presence, and I left our visit feeling calm, peaceful, and confident in both our renewed friendship and my faith. I couldn't wait to leverage, apply, and expand upon this experience each and every day of my life – from that day forward.

This was definitely one of the callings I was seeking to experience in India.

From Marilyn's, I traveled to Pondi and started planning my next trip to Kanyakumari. I asked the ticket agent for help booking the transportation. While working out my details, another customer arrived and asked for travel help. This man was Caucasian and had coloring on his forehead. While we waited for the paperwork, we chatted about our travels in India. He mentioned that he had hired a moped for the day to visit Auroville, which I had not heard of. He was eager to describe the city and offered to take me.

I only hesitated for a moment, thinking I must be crazy to venture with this stranger on his moped to a place I had never heard of.

He told me that his name was Hervé, and he was from France. Like me, he'd worked in the travel industry. He was a former meeting planner/tour guide for the high-end incentive market. He was now living between India and the United States, hoping to bring spiritual tours to India.

A decision that seemed completely irrational turned out to be one of the best experiences of my life. I can't believe I almost missed it.

Auroville is a town where people come together from all countries, religions, and lifestyles to live in united harmony. The town was a vision of "The Mother" from Sri Aurobindo Ashram. She envisioned a town where the inhabitants would celebrate their unity and where everyone would have a spiritual vocation.

Hervé explained that it was similar to Esalen in Big Sur, California, where visitors can relax and experience a more spiritual and connected vacation. Some people eventually choose to live there. He explained that my friends in the New Age and/or yoga world would know of this town.

The main attraction in Auroville is the Matrimandir, which means Temple of the Mother in Sanskrit. The Matrimandir is a large sphere that is gold on the outside and stark white on the inside, with a gigantic crystal in the center. People set up yoga mats, chant, and pray. At first, I thought to myself, "Is this a cult? What have I gotten myself into?" Then I reminded myself that there is one God, and I prayed to Him in the silence.

It was one of the most spiritual experiences I've ever had. I am thankful for another lesson in being open, trusting the unknown, and connecting to humanity.

After Auroville, I traveled to Kanyakumari on the southernmost point of India's peninsula. It is the meeting place of three waterways: the Bay of Bengal, the Arabian Sea, and the Indian Ocean. Kanyakumari holds an importance in the Hindu world as a pilgrim center, but it is also famous for its beautiful views of sunrises and sunsets over the water.

On my first morning in Kanyakumari, I set my alarm for 5:30 a.m. I did not want to miss the sunrise. As I made my way to the beach in the dark, I walked among families headed to the see the sunrise.

The presiding deity that was facing back towards the city was Devi Parasakthi, a virgin goddess in meditative mood. It is written that the lifelike image with a smiling face is a combination of innocence, purity, and beauty. Smeared with sandal paste, decked with different varieties of valuable ornaments, and decorated with beautiful garlands of flowers, she creates a sense of devotion and "peace that passes all understanding" in the mind of every worshipper.

My time in Kanyakumari was quiet and reflective. It reminded me that life has a natural order: the sun rises and sets, the seasons change, the planets rotate, and we control none of it. The universe knows the proper order.

So why did I continue to think that I could control things in life? I pushed and pushed and pushed to make life work the way I wanted it to. And many times in my life, the controlling part of me got in the way of things.

Each and every day in India, I was reminded that I was not in control. Every day, I reassessed my plans based on the situation at that given moment. There was no time to look back or ahead. I had to make decisions based only on the current circumstances, and it took all of my energy.

Kanyakumari brought me back full circle to my reasons for coming to India and what I sought to discover there. One objective was learning to actively apply new behaviors and to respond to life with a more peaceful outlook, with less attachment. I also wanted to completely suspend judgement regarding right or wrong thoughts.

After Kanyakumari, I traveled to Mysore and spent four wonderful days practicing yoga and expanding my spirituality. I learned to be still, to mediate, and to move my body. So, after my time there, it was only natural that I traveled to Rishikesh, known as the World Capital of Yoga.

I was very lucky to stay at the Parmarth Niketan Ashram in Rishikesh during Kumbh Mela, which is the largest religious gathering in the world. It brings Hindu holy men together to discuss their faith and disseminate information about their religion. Pilgrims dip in the holy Ganges River on certain auspicious dates to wash away their sins. The majority of the bathing takes place at the Har-ki-pauri ghat. The next auspicious date was three days after I arrived in Rishikesh. I was going to get a chance to swim in the Ganges with the swamis and cleanse myself. I was listening, and God was providing.

While in Rishikesh, I decided to take a self-designed yoga pilgrimage. I participated in the ashram's Kundalini yoga and meditation classes. Kundalini, the yoga of awareness, awakens the kundalini, which is the unlimited potential that already exists within every human being. My stay at the ashram included private accommodations, three simple meals (a combination of rice, bread, dal, morning chai, potatoes, carrots, and cucumbers), morning Sun Salutation yoga, afternoon Kundalini, then meditation after aarti.

I was planning on staying in Rishikesh the remainder of my stay in India. Being at the foothills of the Himalayas seemed very poetic, bringing my travels full circle. Remembering my life-changing experience in Nepal,

I thought about staying longer and waiting for the weather to clear so I could trek into the mountains from the other side. This thought played through my mind as I sat in lotus position at the end of the Kundalini yoga session each night while the teacher played "May the Longtime Sun." The song seemed to be a sign. It spoke about the sun shining on you and the light around and within you. The final words made me feel like I was in the right place to make another pilgrimage. As I thought about Bishnu and our days spent trekking the Himalayas, the words of the song seemed to speak directly to me. "Guide your way home." It confirmed I needed to make the trek.

However, if Emma Stone played me in my life's movie, she would definitely earn an Oscar for the next part of the film…

On Sunday, April 12, just over two months after I arrived in India, I felt very confident in my ability to be a great traveler. The weather was nice, so I put on my sneakers and set out for a walk. I had read in my travel book about a restaurant called Green Italian, located in the marketplace. I was ready for something different, and I wanted to fulfill my craving for something from home with a pasta meal.

I walked into the restaurant and instantly felt transported to Italy with its red checkered tablecloths and cool fans. Then I looked out the window and saw the cow in the street. Nope! Still in India.

I chose the penne with spinach, olive oil, and parmesan cheese. And a lemon soda. All safe choices in my mind. I ate every forkful, stopping halfway through to write in my journal, *best meal in India!* I finished my meal, paid my check with a large tip because I was so happy, and set out to watch the sunset.

About an hour later, my stomach started flipping and making unusual noises. I thought it was best to head back to my room. I turned away from the sunset and started walking at a normal pace. The growls became louder. I picked up my pace, glad to be wearing my sneakers, and began a mixture of run/walk.

I had been gifted many diarrhea and stomach medicines before leaving for India. And through the nine weeks leading up to that day, I had marveled at how I'd escaped the infamous Delhi belly.

Within two hours, my butt was attached to the toilet and the "fun" didn't stop for another sixteen hours. Not only was I attacked in the rear… oh… I got it good! I also vomited non-stop for sixteen hours. It was the scariest and most nerve-racking experience I've ever had.

I was alone in India, in an ashram. I didn't know anyone and had no way of getting help. I lay in bed crying and puking into a bucket. The walk from my bed to the bathroom was about ten running steps, but I couldn't always make it. I strategically placed another bucket between my bed and the bathroom door.

I know this possibly falls under the category of TMI, but I feel the lowest part of my travels needs to be shared.

I had fluids bursting from every direction. It was painful. I felt very alone. I just cried. I cried out to God, my mother, and everyone I knew to bring me strength in my most vulnerable time.

After the initial sixteen-hour onslaught, I cleaned myself off and walked down the stairs, along the path, and out the gates of the ashram to the Swami-ji Charitable Hospital. It took every ounce of my energy to get there. Looking back, of all the places I stayed in India, being at an ashram that had medical services was a blessing. Even in my lowest of times, I tried to find and see where God provided for me. Those moments saved my sanity.

I saw the doctor. He didn't seem as alarmed as I wanted him to be. He said I had contracted a bacterial infection in my intestines.

"Is that bad?"

In true Indian form, he said, "No problem! This happens all the time. Take a few of these nausea pills and ayurvedic herbs, and you'll be fine in a few days!"

A few days?! He did not hear the words shouting in my head. A few days. I could not do this. I needed to be home. I was wishing, like Dorothy in the Wizard of Oz, that if I just clicked my flip-flops together three times, repeating, "There's no place like home," that I would be there.

I was scheduled to be in India another ten days, but I knew at this point that I was *done!* Getting home became my obsession. At any cost! Sort of…

That was Sunday afternoon. On Thursday, I finally got to an internet café to buy new plane tickets and to send my parents an email: "Hope you are having fun in Disney with Deanna and the kids! Good news… I'm coming home early. Bummer news… I'm really sick!"

My mother replied. "Hi Julie. Got your email about your being sick and returning to Florida early. How are you? Did you get some medicine? How many days were you sick? Let me know how you are and where you are and what kind of medical help you got. Please keep in touch… I will be there to get you on Tuesday at Orlando. Let me know how you are… I am so, so worried about you, and I miss you terribly. May your guardian angel, Athena, be on duty for a few more days. Love you. God be with you. Love, Mom."

I cried and cried and cried. I was crying due to being sick and exhausted, but also because no matter how alone I felt at times, my family – my beautiful, loving, unconditionally supportive family – never failed to be there for me, even halfway around the world.

Getting a new airline ticket was the easy part. Getting myself home was not.

First, there was an eight-hour taxi ride. Forget how much that cost – it was worth it because of the stops on the side of the road to relieve my still very loose bowels. Then I flew to Dubai – four hours with a three-hour layover. Then from Dubai to Washington, DC. An active volcano was erupting over Europe, which added time to my travels. So, the Dubai-to-DC trip took fifteen hours. I missed my connection to DC, so I waited another four hours before finally getting on the plane. Finally, I took the two-hour flight to Orlando.

In Orlando, my mother waited for me with balloons, flowers, and a sign that read "Welcome Home!"

Then we cried. And we cried. And we cried. Tears of joy, relief, concern, and love. There were tears, and tears, and tears, and tears. And we had the longest hug ever. I was home! God bless America and moms!

After what I thought would only be two weeks of recovering, my concerned parents, my medical professionals, and my body came to the conclusion that I could not return to my life in San Francisco.

I was disappointed, but not upset. During my ten weeks in India, I'd had the opportunity to take time away from my everyday life, time by myself to think. When I'd lost my job in 2008, I thought I had lost my dream job. I'd been so excited work with people and coach them in their careers within the company, and I felt deflated when I was let go. But I was also a little mad. There I was, investing in a career as a coach, and I didn't have a job in which to use my new certification and skills. That situation led me to the volunteer opportunity with CCS, which led me to have a clear head to recalculate my life while I was in India. In many situations, I learned to adapt to what I needed to do next to move forward. My health setback didn't derail me from my future. Instead, it helped me be clear about what I wanted to do. I wanted to teach and coach people, and I needed to travel. I didn't need a dream job; I wanted a dream life.

One Sunday, when I was starting to feel better, my mom asked if I would like to go to church with her. Immediately I answered, "Yes. But I am not feeling up to the traditional church." I had been raised going to Catholic school, and my family belonged to a traditional Roman Catholic church, though we had always promoted spirituality over dogma. Also, honoring all that I experienced in India, I wanted to be with a group of people whom I believed to be more transcendent.

My mom found an ad for a Unity church in the newspaper, and it was not far from her home. The announcement stated that a local musician named Elaine Silver would be participating in the service.

"Elaine Silver?" my mother said. "Mrs. Silver had a daughter named Elaine, and she was a musician. I wonder if this is the same Elaine?"

"Mom, why would Mrs. Silver's daughter be in Florida?" Mrs. Silver was my nursery schoolteacher in Pine Brook, New Jersey. What were the chances of her daughter being at a church in Florida?

My mom picked up the phone and called the church. "Is there any chance the singer, Elaine Silver, is from New Jersey?"

The voice on the other end of the phone confirmed that, in fact, Elaine was from New Jersey and now lived in Sarasota.

We got ready and headed to church. After the service, we found Elaine. My mother introduced us, explaining that my siblings and I had attended nursery school with her mother, who'd been our teacher. Elaine was thrilled, and we exchanged contact information.

By May, I was feeling better, and I was ready to go back to San Francisco despite not having any job leads.

"I need to get back to my life!" I announced to no one.

When I got to San Francisco, my friend Michelle, who ran a boat tour company in Lake Tahoe, asked me if I would be open to a business opportunity. In exchange for free rent, I would help with childcare in the mornings and work on the boat in the afternoons. Since my trek through the Himalayan foothills was cut short by my illness, the idea of spending the summer in the mountains was enticing.

While working and having fun in Lake Tahoe, I had downtime to once again recalculate what mattered most to me. I knew I liked coaching, and I wasn't interested in going back into the corporate world. I wanted to start my own business. I realized that San Francisco would no longer be affordable. I liked living in Florida, which was more conducive to an entrepreneurial lifestyle. So, in August, when my services were no longer needed in Lake Tahoe, I said goodbye to the West Coast once again and headed back to Florida.

I didn't have many friends except for my mother, my father and his wife, and a few aunts and uncles. I remembered having Elaine Silver's contact information, and I sent her an email.

Elaine's automated response informed me that she was on a summer musical tour. The email was signed:

Elaine Silver
Reverend
Fairy
Musician
Passion Test Facilitator

I passed right over the musician and fairy and stopped at Passion Test Facilitator. What is the Passion Test? I researched it on the internet. What I found was a video of Janet Attwood, the creator of the Passion Test, talking about the process and how to get certified:

The Passion Test is a simple, powerful set of tools for discovering your passions and aligning your life with what matters most to you. The Passion Test shows you, step by step, how to identify your top five passions, then provides the guidance to align your life with these passions.

This was exactly what I wanted to help people do! I didn't have my own tools to share yet, so I, too, needed to be a Certified Passion Test Facilitator! I signed up right then. Two months later, I was certified in Calgary, Canada by Janet Attwood. Eleven years later, I still use the Passion Test with my clients, and I'm a Master Trainer who gets to travel the world training other trainers on how to facilitate this life-changing process. Thank you, Janet!

REFLECTION ON R: 7 STEPS TO RECALCULATE YOUR EXTRAORDINARY LIFE

WHAT STORY ARE you still telling yourself about why you can't have or achieve what you truly desire? You're not alone in those thoughts.

We've all done it: put our happiness on hold until some magical future date when maybe we can give ourselves permission to finally be happy.

People like me who are living a satisfying and fulfilling life know the answers to three questions:

- What do you really want?
- What's preventing you from having it?
- How do you change your life now?

If you can't answer these three questions right now, The Travelers H.E.A.R.T. will show you how.

As a certified Master Trainer of the Passion Test created by Janet Attwood and Chris Attwood, as well as a Strategic Intervention Coach with Robbins-Madanes Training, I learned the benefit of following specific systems and steps for creating lasting change. (If it works for renowned transformational leaders like Janet Attwood and Tony Robbins, it can work for you and me.)

My Seven Miracle Steps is a sequence of actions steps. When you understand and master what must be done to break through old behavioral and thought patterns, you can begin to think and live differently. You can finally experience the life of your dreams, visions, and desires.

HERE ARE THE SEVEN MIRACLE STEPS:

Step 1: Magnify what's missing that is most important to you.
Step 2: Investigate your current thoughts and emotions.
Step 3: Replace the negative with a magical incantation.
Step 4: Attend to your passions with inspired action.
Step 5: Create a promise for your compelling future.
Step 6: Let go of the "how."
Step 7: Enjoy the process as much as the achievement.

STEP 1: MAGNIFY WHAT'S MISSING THAT IS MOST IMPORTANT TO YOU.

Reflect on what matters most to you and write it down. Sounds simple and obvious, right? Do you know how many people have never done this? Too many!

There is no better tool on the planet for getting clear on what matters most to you than The Passion Test System, created by Janet Attwood and Chris Attwood. Since 2010, I have been using this tool for clients and myself. As a Master Trainer and Facilitator of this highly effective and life-changing process, I have witnessed its impact on people all over the world.

Let's get started. Grab a piece of paper and write at the top, "When my life is ideal, I am…"

Next comes the fun part. Close your eyes and spend a few moments in silence, listening to your heart. What does it want for you? Got it?

Now create a list of ten or fifteen things that you want to experience. Be sure to include all areas of your life, including relationships, career, family, hobbies, spirituality, health and well-being, finances, environment, being in service, friends, and of course, travel.

STEP 2: INVESTIGATE YOUR CURRENT THOUGHTS AND EMOTIONS THAT RULE YOUR WORLD.

Notice the negative or disempowering words, thoughts, and beliefs that currently stop you from acting on what is most important to you. List them.

I highly recommend taking the Energy Leadership Index assessment, otherwise known as the ELI, to support Step 2. People are often unaware of how unconscious thoughts and perceptions influence their emotions, thoughts, and actions. As a certified iPEC Coach since 2009, I have all my clients take this powerful assessment so they can see for themselves where their negative and limiting thoughts hold them back from experiencing greater success and more joy.

STEP 3: REPLACE THE NEGATIVE WITH A MAGICAL INCANTATION.

Using the list above, circle the word, thought, or belief that you use most often or that is your biggest challenge. Now, think of a word, statement, or incantation that is uplifting, empowering, and inspiring.

For example, if your thought is "I'm not smart enough," replace it with something bold and sassy like "I'm brilliant and I know it. I got this."

STEP 4: ATTEND TO YOUR PASSIONS WITH INSPIRED ACTION.

Now that you are clear about what matters most to you, it is your job to place positive attention on those things every day. Remember, the more you give attention and power to something, the stronger and more expansive it gets. Living in a culture of competing interests and distractions, you must stay intentional with your attention. This is the only way you will attract blessings and miracles in your life.

STEP 5: CREATE A PROMISE FOR YOUR COMPELLING FUTURE.

A promise is a commitment to provide a particular future or outcome. So, while we dream of a promising future, we must act on that promise today.

In Step 5, you must first write what you promise to fully commit to without excuse. Then, you must get clear on why you are making the promise. Only when you have a compelling why will you take consistent, inspired action. Finally, know what is at stake. What will be the cost of you *not* following through or keeping your promise? How you show up today will directly impact your future.

STEP 6: LET GO OF THE "HOW."

Any question starting with "how" can only be answered by past experiences, leaving no room for progress, innovation, or new possibilities. To create and experience a compelling future, start asking "What?" with genuine curiosity right now. Better questions generate better results.

- What challenges are you facing right now?
- What opportunities do you see?
- What else?
- What action can you take now?
- What is stopping you?
- What support do you need?

STEP 7: ENJOY THE PROCESS AS MUCH AS THE ACHIEVEMENT.

The magic and miracles constantly happen when you are fully present in the moment. When your mind is filled with regrets of the past or worry of the future, you miss out on blessings of the present. Stay focused on the here and now, celebrating all that is good. Stay open to all that is yet to come your way. Welcome the miracles!

India: Cross Cultural Solutions Volunteer

Julie A. Zolfo

Camel Safari to Pakistan Border with kid guides

Rishikesh, India: Pasta, Parasite & Praying to Mom

Julie A. Zolfo

Always yield to the cow in the street

India with Marilyn, Herv, Susan and the locals

State Speaker to Global Trainer (Passion Test)

WISDOM:
TRUST THAT PLANS ALWAYS CHANGE AND JUST F.L.O.W.

DESIRE:
CO-CREATE

"HOW DID I get here?"

"Seriously, how did I get here?"

The inner dialogue I was having with myself was one-sided because I wasn't getting any answers. I stood in the living room of my new house in Bend. Oregon, surrounded by eighty boxes of *stuff!*

I looked around me. Exactly one year earlier, in March 2020, the world was shut down by a global pandemic. I had just gotten back from a work cruise and was on a high from all that was accomplished with a great group of women. I returned home to my townhouse, where I stayed in quarantine for months, as did the rest of the world. I got to know those walls and ceilings pretty well.

Now, in March 2021, I was surrounded by new walls and new ceilings. A new fireplace. A new kitchen. A great room. A master suite. A guest bedroom, an office, a two-car garage, and a backyard. All my own.

"How did I get here?"

The other half of my brain started to wake up and respond to my questions.

"Wow! How did I get here? A homeowner!"

"I remember traveling the world with a backpack for nine months. A backpack! Now I have a guest bedroom!"

"Yes. The adventure trips through Southeast Asia, India, Europe, Costa Rica, and Peru felt like a lifetime ago. But that isn't how I got here. *This* here. This standing right here. This started with my transformation in 2010. It was after India."

I stopped talking to myself and sat down to think. I wanted to know exactly how I'd gotten here – a life filled with flow and ease – and how I could coach others to get to a similar place. Obviously, there was something bigger at play…

Most people know that change is the only constant, and that life is always asking us to adapt, but there is often resistance.

A traveler, on the other hand, fully embraces that change, transition, and the unknown will be part of their experience. Fundamentally, travel helps people pursue what is on the other side of change.

Sometimes the change is self-imposed, and sometimes it imposes itself on you. There are times when change is welcomed with open arms – like a new job, a new relationship, or a new family member. Sometimes change is met with a stiff arm as you push it away with great force. These situations may include a new condescending boss, an unforeseen break-up, or the sudden loss of a family member. Or a world pandemic.

A study by American Express titled "Life Twists" confirmed the increasing need for adaptability and flexibility amid the twists and turns of life in this accelerating digital world. In its findings, 95% of Americans surveyed agreed that the road to a satisfying life likely involves detours, delays, and unexpected changes. Additionally, 94% of those folks said being open to change is a key component in experiencing a more fulfilling life.

Just because they know it, are they really open to change? Are you?

How often do you go with the flow?

Everyone seemed to master going with the flow except me. Just go with the flow… It sounds so simple, right? What was getting in my way? I wanted life to be easygoing and to be less emotionally impacted when life changed directions expectantly. But it did not come naturally to me.

The solution to my "flow dilemma" finally struck me years later – after a long period of not traveling. I was living in Florida, a state I said I would never, ever live in. Until that point, I believed the term "go with the flow" was a bit hippy-dippy. I thought it meant having no plan at all. However, I learned that my belief was not true.

As I sat on the beach looking at the Gulf of Mexico, I concluded that going with the flow doesn't mean not having a plan. Rather, it's about not being attached to the plan. (Like we say in the Passion Test process, "This or something better.") Ironically, I can look back on my life now and acknowledge that I did, indeed, trust that the plan always changes. I was going with it for years; I was just calling it life!

With my new perspective on the word "flow," I saw that I had unconsciously picked up a few more insights while on the road. These unspoken decrees not only made life as a traveler more fluid and flexible, but they also played a large role in navigating life's ongoing changes with increased fun, freedom, and fascination.

So here is my version of F.L.O.W. and how I leverage its directives to keep me afloat on the road and at home:

FOCUS ON THE CALM, NOT THE CHAOS.
Early in my travel days, I learned two golden rules to live by when my travels appeared to go sideways (which happened often). First, see things for what they are, but not worse than what they are. Second, seek out the opportunity in an unplanned circumstance rather than complaining about the crisis or challenge. These practices were both so valuable, I combined them into one idea: focus on the calm, not the chaos.

LISTEN IN STILLNESS TO THE SILENCE. IT HAS SOMETHING TO SAY.
The first time I heard silence was on my trek through the Himalayas. I was resting on a mountain ledge, sipping hot lemon tea from my thermos. As

I sat there, captivated by the snow wisping off the white-capped mountains, the whispers of my soul called to me. Ever since then, I have made it a priority to sit in stillness daily. And when there is a conflict between my head and my heart, I find the tie-breaking solution while sitting in silence, every time.

OBSERVE AND OBEY LIFE'S NATURAL SEASONS AND CYCLES.

Spring. Summer. Fall. Winter. Repeat. Each season is beautiful, serves a purpose, and completes a cycle of change and transformation. Much like the change of seasons, it's imperative to embrace all changes as a gift and an invitation to play out what is needed: a time to start, a time to celebrate, a time to release, a time to die. What season of life are you in now? Are you accepting it or resisting it? To grow and flow through life's inevitable ups and downs, we must move with and through each season of life.

WELCOME GOODBYES AND HELLOS ALIKE.

One of the biggest joys of travel for me is the rotation of new faces that come in and out of my day. Some people I meet on the bus for a few hours, while others stick around for days or maybe weeks after sharing a bonding experience over a hike, a meal, or a smile. The effortless ebb and flow makes it easy drop in and out with other travelers without resentment, judgement, or guilt. I learned, and still appreciate, the freedom to say goodbye or hello at any time while traveling. Applying this guidance to dating, relationships, jobs, or even the death of a loved one takes practice. But it's important to apply all the same.

Listen to the silence. Something I had not remembered until 2017, when I had a time to stop and take a breath while living by myself in Dallas, Texas. After I left India in 2010, I lived in Florida, South Carolina, North Carolina, and Texas. I went to Dallas because it was close to a hub and a training center. My job was remote, so moving to Dallas seemed completely logical, a great career move. Once there, I found that there weren't any opportunities there after all. Nothing about Dallas was for me – no family, no friends, and no nature. I was ready to move again.

It was time to look outside of the company, and I scoured a job search engine for positions in Denver, San Diego, and Bend, Oregon. Why not move near my brother and his family? I loved Oregon every time I visited them. It was the perfect travel destination with mountains to climb and plenty of open space filled with silence. And that is where the most intriguing job opportunity appeared.

I was perfectly qualified. It was a coaching position, and the candidate needed iPEC certification. That was me! But they wanted someone already living in Bend, and I couldn't leave for three months.

I wasn't too upset about not getting the job, but I thought, "That is where I want to be!" So, I moved again. Sight unseen. I had to go with the flow, trusting that my mother had my best interest at heart when she found a townhouse in Bend for me while visiting my brother and his wife. I loved it so much, I lived there for three years.

Bend turned out to be the perfect destination to fuel my Traveler's Heart. There are mountains to trek, people with the same mindset, and family. Being there has allowed me to breathe among the trees and be at peace with the inner me.

And that is how I got to living in my new house in 2021.

REFLECTION ON T: WHAT DOES IT MEAN TO TRUST F.L.O.W.?

ARE YOU LIVING in the F.L.O.W. of your life? Being able to move into a flow state is positively life changing. It offers the stability to stay in peace, even when pieces of your life fall to the ground.

Below are some questions to consider when assessing your current flow state and ways you can improve upon it.

- Where in your life could you benefit from being less controlling and more allowing of your circumstances?
- What actions can you take that would bring you back to a place of peace when life appears to fall to pieces?
- Where in your life can you celebrate the progress, you have made rather focusing on what you have not yet achieved or completed?
- How will it benefit you to practice trust and flow more consistently in at least one area of your life?
- What is it costing you (mentally, emotionally, financially, spiritually, physically) by not trusting that circumstances will work out in your favor?

Julie A. Zolfo

My Happy Feet Moments with and without a passport

Pre-trip wisdom and love from my parents

Bend, OR: Three Sisters Wilderness Day hike

26 WAYS TO KEEP YOUR TRAVELER'S HEART BEATING EVERYDAY

(A TO M)

APPRECIATE everything you are and what you have right now.
BELIEVE in your abilities, capabilities, and possibilities.
CONNECT to learn about another, not to brag about yourself.
DARE to do life differently, without approval or apologizes.
EXPERIENCE life curiously, freely, and openly.
FOCUS on the contributions, not the circumstances.
GROUND your thoughts and emotions with gratitude daily.
HONOR the whispers calling you from your heart.
INTEND only the best outcome for others and yourself.
JOYFULLY accept that what is, is exactly what is best for you.
KISS culturally as a sign of recognition and reverence.
LAUGH at yourself more, so others can laugh with you, too.
MOMENTS, not money, yield a rich life.

26 WAYS TO KEEP YOUR TRAVELER'S HEART BEATING EVERYDAY

(N TO Z)

NURTURE your body, mind, and spirit by spending time in nature.
OPEN-MINDEDNESS allows for inquiry before a conclusion.
PASSIONATELY engage in everything you do.
QUIET the mind deliberately, so you can act decisively.
RISK following where your heart wants to lead you, every time.
SAY thank you, please forgive me, I'm sorry, and I love you first.
TRUST in the divine's perfect timing, intervention, and guidance.
UNDERSTAND others more than they understand themselves.
VIEW everyone you meet as a teacher.
WANDER outside your comfort zone, willingly.
XEROX only the documents that prove you are an original.
YES, absolutely yes, creates infinite possibilities for miracles.
ZERO% is required of you for the universe to love you 100%.

UNPACK YOUR TRAVELER'S H.E.A.R.T.

"A mind that stretched by new experiences can never go back to its old dimensions."

~Oliver Wendel Homes, Jr.

THANK YOU FOR traveling with me through the many mountains – real and metaphorical – in my life so far. My wish is that you travel more and feel inspired to traverse the inner adversaries and outward adventures of your own life. Your Traveler's Heart will never lead you astray.

I know this to be true: to achieve an extraordinary life, you must take new steps in a different direction. You must be willing to explore what you don't know so you experience the full spectrum of life's joys, setbacks, and setups. This practice will ultimately lead you beyond what you imagine for yourself. I promise!

Travel is *the* quintessential vehicle to access the five desires: Connection, Curiosity, Courage, Clarity, and Co-Creation. Think of travel as purchasable wisdom and transformation. As a result of your investment, you experience more freedom, more possibilities, and more change with an open heart, an inquiring mind, and happier feet.

We all have a traveler living inside of us whose sole purpose is to help us escape from what we know so we can see life from a different perspective. How you choose to harness that new information is entirely up to you.

Here's the thing… the same level of thinking that has brought you this far won't take you where you want to go next. Luckily, you've landed here with me, where you can get the expert guidance you need to veer off the tried-and-true trails and turn onto a newer path of possibilities – a path you don't need to travel alone!

Julie Zolfo

TRANSITION COACH | TRAINER | SPEAKER

ABOUT THE AUTHOR

WHEN YOU SUMMIT a mountain, there is a surge of energy, and you feel as if you are on the top of the world. That is also what you feel when you meet Julie Zolfo, a world traveler, certified transformational coach, and a force of energy.

With her energy, travel know-how, and over thirty years of coaching, recruiting, training, and leadership experience, Julie inspires those who have lost sight of their unique gifts, heart's desires, and self-worth, by opening the doors of empowerment and transformation. Her clients learn to take the necessary leap to reclaim their joy and meaning again in their lives.

Julie has been her own client and created for herself five grounding factors that she has coined her Five Fs - Faith, Family, Food, Fun, and Football. These five grounding factors have enabled her to fly higher in her career and personal life, living out dreams and wishes most people are too afraid to explore or even take a first step towards achieving - she used this to summit many mountains - her highest peak was in Nepal.

Julie encourages her coaching clients to find their own letter sequence. In fact, Julie added a sixth F, Feet when she created the life concept, The Happy Feet Mindset.

When following her career path, Julie acquired notable coaching certifications including Strategic Intervention Coach from Madanes-Robbins Coaching, a Tony Robbins endorsed program, her Master Energy Leadership Coach from iPEC and most recently earned the title Master

Trainer within the Passion Test Process under Janet Attwood, New York Times Bestselling Co-Author and the creator of Passion Test and Master of Self Love. It was during her own training in 2010 with the Passion Test, Julie had a deeply transformative experience that led her to develop her Fulfillment Factor Formula™ process. In 2011 & 2012, Julie's proprietary coaching process was published in two self-help Amazon compilation best-sellers.

In 2011, Julie established her coaching business by consciously leveraging travel and the great outdoors as her go-to vehicle to support her clients. She helps them create and sustain life-altering changes in their careers, relationships, health, and finances. Intuitively, Julie combined her twenty-plus years of human performance and talent development expertise while employed at some of the most prestigious global companies such as Deloitte, Honeywell, Citigroup, and Turner Broadcasting Sales. Combined with her coaching certifications and her passion for experimental travel, Julie created an unrivaled coaching approach, The Traveler's H.E.A.R.T.

Today, Julie is based in the majestic and magical mountain town Bend, Oregon, where she enjoys hiking, kayaking, and family time while offering outdoor coaching, workshops, and Elite VIP to her clients from around the globe when she is not traveling to her corporate clients or at a speaking engagement. If you are finally ready to move beyond what is not working and really want to reimagine what is more possible for your career, your business and personal life, visit Julie's website to book a BIG LEAP call with her.

www.juliezolfo.com

www.ingramcontent.com/pod-product-compliance
Lightning Source LLC
LaVergne TN
LVHW011834060526
838200LV00053B/4012